Chicago Guide
to Preparing
Electronic Manuscripts

Chicago Guides
to *Writing*, Editing,
and Publishing

Chicago Guide
to Preparing
Electronic Manuscripts

FOR AUTHORS AND PUBLISHERS

The University of Chicago Press

Chicago

The University of Chicago Press, Chicago 60637
The University of Chicago Press, Ltd., London

Library of Congress Cataloging-in-Publication Data

Chicago guide to preparing electronic manuscripts
  for authors and publishers.

  (Chicago guides to writing, editing, and publishing)
  Bibliography: p. 131
  Includes index.
  1. Electronic publishing—Handbooks, manuals, etc.
2. Manuscript preparation (Authorship)—Handbooks,
manuals, etc.   3. Authorship—Data processing—
Handbooks, manuals, etc.   4. Publishers and publishing—
Data processing—Handbooks, manuals, etc.
I. University of Chicago Press.   II. Series.
Z286.E43C48   1987   070.5'028'5   86-19343
ISBN 0-226-10392-7
ISBN 0-226-10393-5 (pbk.)

Contents

Preface

A manuscript prepared by an author on a computer and submitted to a publisher on disk or tape—termed an "electronic manuscript" by the publishing industry—can be used for setting type without rekeyboarding, and sometimes for other purposes. This guide is addressed to authors and publishers who wish to use electronic manuscripts for typesetting. Since the techniques for producing camera-ready copy are different from those for converting a manuscript from one device to another, this guide does not give instructions on how to use equipment like the laser printers now available for use with computers. In this guide we presuppose that the goal is to produce a professionally designed book selecting from the full range of typefaces and type sizes available from full-service typesetters. The suggestions offered here follow the progress of a book manuscript from first typing to page proof and index and show what author and publisher can do to help realize the benefits offered by electronic manuscripts, such as the possibility of reduced proofreading and lower typesetting costs.

Since 1981 the University of Chicago Press has been accepting electronic manuscripts and producing typeset proof directly from magnetic media supplied by authors. Much of what we know about text processing we have learned by trial and error. We hope to reduce your trials and help you to avert errors by passing on these observations from our learning experience. Our solutions took no great investment in equipment but did require a serious commitment of time and a willingness to learn. We think that others can use the methods outlined here to make good use of the computer technology of the 1980s in the service of honored traditions of bookmaking.

Authors using computers can follow this guide even if they are not certain who will eventually publish the resulting book. Publishers who enjoy the cooperation of their authors and typesetters can make use of these procedures even if they have no computer equipment themselves. Much of the advice in this guide can also be used by publishers with in-house text editing systems. Our focus is on manuscript preparation—how it should be done when computers are used—and on the procedures that should be followed by author and publisher so that the author's electronic medium can be used for typesetting. Although it has been in the production of books that the authors of this guide have gained their experience, the advice herein should be helpful to the authors and publishers of journal and magazine articles and other publishing products as well. We give examples of the mnemonic codes in use at the Press, but the procedures described here could be used with other coding schemes.

When our authors first asked us for advice on how to prepare their electronic manuscripts, we passed such queries on to our typesetters. Soon it became clear that authors needed advice before the work was ready for typesetting, often even before the work was accepted for publication. With the encouragement of the director, Morris Philipson, the staff of the University of Chicago Press undertook to learn how the new technologies would affect the publishing process. The Press decided to investigate various approaches rather than experiment with any particular text editing system. Jennie Lightner, senior manuscript editor, and Pamela Pokorney, senior production controller, were principally involved with that investigation. Until the volume of electronic manuscripts became too large, Lightner and Pokorney handled all such projects, gaining firsthand experience and at the same time following the experiences of other publishers through trade journals, workshops, and conferences. They wrote the original guidelines for authors of electronic manuscripts that were distributed to Press authors, and they have now expanded them into this book for more general use. The instruction given in chapter 1—not to use the letter "el" when the number "one" is intended—comes from one who labored through a long manuscript changing an author's "els" to "ones." Other advice in this guide comes from similar experience.

We owe a debt of gratitude to all the authors who cooperated in the development of procedures for handling electronic manuscripts for their willingness to add coding and editing and for commenting on our guidelines. Also, many present and former colleagues from the staff of the Press and the University of Chicago Printing Department deserve special thanks for their comments and suggestions, including Penny Kaiserlian, Joe Alderfer, Alice Bennett, Robert Berg, Jean Eckenfels, Margaret Flack Mahan, Claudia Rex, Virginia Seidman, Catharine Seybold, Wendy Strothman, and Bruce Young. The Press is grateful to the Computation Center of the University of Chicago for its commitment to the education of Press staff on text processing and computer technology. Our thanks are given in particular to lead staff analyst Joel J. Mambretti, Information Technologies and New Services, who has patiently answered our technical questions, in English, and whose sensible suggestions have saved the day more than once.

We also express our gratitude to the typesetters and other suppliers who gave freely of their knowledge to help us solve problems. We are indebted particularly to Eileen Cohen of Carlisle Graphics, Dubuque, Iowa, formerly of the University of Chicago Printing Department, to William M. Grosskopf and Richard Workman of G & S Typesetters, Austin, Texas, and to Judith Pritchard and Scott Woodhall of Chas. P. Young, Chicago.

Special thanks are due to Stan McCracken for his careful reading of an earlier draft and the constructive comments that resulted therefrom.

Portions of this book have been adapted from *The Chicago Manual of Style,* 13th edition, © 1969, 1982 by The University of Chicago.

Electronic processing is a continuously developing technology, and new ways of using the technology are constantly being devised. We plan to revise and update this guide regularly, as new information and improved techniques are developed, and we welcome any suggestions from readers for its improvement. Suggestions and questions should be sent to the Editor, *Chicago Guide to Preparing Electronic Manuscripts,* University of Chicago Press, 5801 South Ellis Avenue, Chicago, IL 60637 U.S.A.

Introduction

Electronic manuscripts have been making their way into publishers' consciousness over the past few years, as more and more authors choose to prepare their manuscripts on computers. Statistics published in 1984 by the Association of American Publishers confirm that authors have been ahead of publishers in the electronic revolution: while more than 80 percent of the authors surveyed by the AAP indicated that they would be using computers for manuscript preparation by 1985, the publishers surveyed estimated that fewer than 50 percent of authors would do so. Both authors and publishers agreed, though, that their use of electronic technology for manuscript preparation and processing would increase over the next five years.

The value of word processing to authors is already well documented. Less has been written about how publishers can make use of authors' electronic manuscripts for typesetting and other purposes, although it is commonly assumed that this is easy to do. Authors' keystrokes have proved harder to capture than publishers first supposed at the beginning of the 1980s. With cooperation between author and publisher, however, the elusive keystrokes can be captured and reused. It is the purpose of this book to give practical guidance to both author and publisher on how to prepare and handle electronic manuscripts for best results. The benefit of lower typesetting costs can be realized only when author and publisher work closely together with full knowledge of their respective tasks. Author, publisher, and customer benefit from lower typesetting costs since such cost savings are usually reflected in a lower price for the book. Another advantage for authors in following these instructions is gaining greater control over the final page proof; although proofreading must still be done at various stages, authors are proofreading their own work rather than that of a typesetter.

After six years of working with electronic manuscripts, we have gained considerable experience with electronic processing and we expect this method to increase in importance as publishers, authors, and typesetters become more familiar with the special requirements of electronic manu-

1

scripts. The University of Chicago Press first converted an electronic manuscript in 1981. For the next two years, to gain more experience in converting electronic manuscripts, the Press converted every manuscript that had been prepared on a computer. In 1982 we received and converted 10 electronic manuscripts; in 1983, 20. In 1984, we began to select more carefully which projects would be converted, on the basis of our growing experience. Although we received more computer-prepared manuscripts than ever before in 1984, we used authors' electronic manuscripts in only 9 cases. In 1985, we stopped counting how many manuscripts were prepared on computers but recorded that we converted 11 electronic manuscripts. In 1986, 17 manuscripts were converted, representing about 15 percent of our list of original titles. Also, the manuscripts of a number of major works in progress are being coded for electronic processing from first preparation.

In this guide we call the traditional methods of handling manuscripts "conventional processing." We call the newer procedures "electronic processing." In conventional manuscript processing, the manuscript is typed by the author or the author's typist, edited by the publisher's copyeditor, and retyped (or "rekeyboarded" in the industry jargon) into the typesetting computer by typesetting personnel. The typesetter produces galley or page proofs, which are proofread by the typesetter, by the author, and often by the publisher. Errors made in rekeyboarding are corrected in another "pass" through the typesetting system, and revised proofs are generated for further checking.

When an author submits a manuscript in electronic form, the files on the magnetic tape or disks are transmitted into the typesetting computer, eliminating the need for rekeyboarding. This idea of "captured keystrokes" is central to electronic processing. If the electronic manuscript has been properly prepared, the typesetter can produce galley or page proofs that may require only spot-checking rather than word-by-word proofreading.

Although the possibilities presented by electronic technology are exciting, some words of caution are in order. Cost savings and reduced proofreading will not be realized unless the manuscript is carefully and consistently prepared at the initial stages. This guide has been designed to help authors prepare manuscripts that take best advantage of the new technology and to help publishers adjust to that technology as well. The procedures outlined here are those in use in the books division of the University of Chicago Press; they represent less an authoritative methodology than a series of steps we have found to be practical and successful. Authors are advised to consult with their own publishers about the specific requirements of a particular house. Publishers are strongly advised to establish consistent procedures and to arrange for a test of a sample electronic medium by a typesetter before encouraging an author to proceed with coding.

It is a rare manuscript that can make its way through the publication process with no need of editing. Because the typeset proofs generated from an electronic manuscript will reproduce what the author has entered, it is important that the electronic medium (disks or magnetic tape) supplied to the typesetter be as final and correct as possible. One must ensure that the publisher's editing changes, as well as the author's revisions, are incorporated into the electronic script. Who will accomplish this is one of the key questions to ask when determining whether a manuscript should be processed electronically.

Various approaches to adding the editing to the electronic medium can be summarized as follows (for full details see chap. 3):

If the publisher lacks an in-house editing system or the requisite staff, or if the author has used equipment not directly compatible with the publisher's system, the publisher may ask the author to add the editorial revisions to the electronic manuscript using the equipment on which the manuscript was originally prepared. Before submitting the tape or disks, the author submits a printout of the manuscript for the publisher to edit. The publisher returns the edited printout to the author for revision of the electronic version. This is the procedure most commonly followed at the Press and is still the most prevalent method in the mid-1980s.

A publisher that has an in-house word processing system, as well as the staff to do the work, may be able to transfer the electronic version of the manuscript to this system and edit it electronically. The author submits a printout together with the tape or disks; the publisher's staff either edits the printout and then updates the electronic version or, in some cases, edits the electronic version on-line, bypassing the intermediate step of editing the printout. The publisher then delivers the fully edited electronic version, with a new printout generated ·by the publisher, to the typesetter. Although at present only a few publishers have fully developed in-house text editing departments, this approach is the most desirable one for publishers who intend to process many electronic manuscripts of a similar type or by the same authors. The publisher retains control over the quality of the electronic manuscript and over the publication schedule as well. For this approach to work, of course, the author must have a system that is compatible with the publisher's or media that can be readily converted to the publisher's requirements.

The typesetter may add the editing. The author submits a printout of the manuscript together with the unedited tape or disks; the publisher edits the printout and sends it, with the unedited tape or disks, to the typesetter. The typesetter updates the electronic files using the computerized composition system. We have found this to be the least economical form of electronic processing; having the typesetter update the electronic files can cost as much as having the typesetter rekeyboard the entire manuscript. Even so, this approach may be worth considering in order to retain the bulk of the author's work and reduce the author's proofreading burden.

Although the Press has entered the editing and coding of a limited number of electronic manuscripts in-house—and finds the in-house approach the ideal one—in the real world of limited resources the Press most frequently uses the first approach and asks the author to add the editing and coding.

Before a manuscript can be sent to a typesetter, different kinds of text elements (chapter openings, block quotations, footnotes) and special characters (Greek and math characters, diacritics) must be identified. In conventional processing this is done through a combination of author styling (the author may type all chapter titles in capitals, for example) and editorial markup (the copyeditor labels each text element and unusual character in the margin of the manuscript while editing the text). In the same way, text elements and special characters in the electronic manuscript need to be identified, so that the typesetter can assign typographic specifications to them. The electronic counterpart to author styling and editorial markup is generic coding. Coding is necessary because the traditional techniques of author styling, such as centering, indenting, and using capital letters, not only do not work well but actually cause problems with electronic processing. Organizational features such as chapter openings, subheadings, and block quotations and special characters such as diacritics, Greek characters, and math symbols must be labeled with a consistent and unique set of codes. Some codes can be typed by the author directly into the manuscript during its initial preparation; others can be added later, after editing by the publisher has been completed. (A summary of industry efforts to standardize generic coding and instructions on generic coding of electronic manuscripts are presented in chap. 2 of this guide.)

In conventional processing a skilled practitioner of typesetting, while typing the text into the typesetting system, examines the author styling and editorial markup and inserts into the text specific, usually very long typesetting codes that will produce the type style and formatting that is desired.

In electronic processing the generic codes inserted by the author or the author's typist are not directly usable by the typesetting system. To produce the type style and formatting that is desired, typesetting personnel must first convert the generic codes to the long, specific codes that the typesetting system recognizes. Such code conversions are *not* automatic. Typesetting personnel must write a program that will convert the very simple, generic codes to very complex typesetting codes. A properly prepared and coded electronic manuscript will allow the programming the typesetter must do to proceed easily and accurately. The programming required by an improperly prepared and coded electronic manuscript will be difficult and error-prone.

This guide is divided into three chapters, the first two addressed to authors, and the third to publishers. However, authors and publishers alike are strongly urged to familiarize themselves with the entire text and not just the portions specifically addressed to them and to resist the temptation to consult it simply as a reference work. Authors looking for instructions on a given topic should keep in mind that chapter 1 discusses manuscript preparation while chapter 2 discusses coding. Hence, for example, authors investigating how to prepare footnotes should consult what is said in chapter 2 on the subject as well as in chapter 1, and vice versa. They should not simply imitate the examples in chapter 1 without first checking that chapter 2 does not have more to say on footnotes—which, of course, it does.

In this guide we often give alternative ways of proceeding. It is terribly important, after deciding which alternative procedure best fits an author's system and the requirements of a particular publisher, that an author stick to that alternative. For example, it is not acceptable sometimes to use the code </p> to indicate paragraph endings and other times to use a carriage return alone (see 1.39). Authors must choose one alternative and use it consistently throughout their manuscripts.

Please note that, for emphasis and because even those readers who initially read this book straight through will eventually consult it as a reference work, certain points are reiterated. These are points that have been found especially important to the preparation process.

1 Instructions to Authors

1.1 Preparing a manuscript for electronic processing requires a change in the way we think about manuscripts. For many years, publishers, including the University of Chicago Press, have provided you—our authors—with guidelines for manuscript preparation that focus on the physical appearance of the manuscript. Such guidelines are intended to apprise you of publishers' requirements and preferences so that the editing, design, production, and eventual publication of your books can take place smoothly, without delay, and without unnecessary repetition of steps. In electronic processing the physical appearance of the printout in many respects takes second place to the care and structural consistency with which the electronic manuscript is prepared as well as to the requirements of the typesetter for a trouble-free conversion of your electronic manuscript to typeset proofs. Despite this shift of emphasis, the intent of this guide is the same as that of other manuscript preparation guides: to provide you and your publisher with advice and instruction so that your book can be published as quickly as possible, without delays caused by improper manuscript preparation.

1.2 Before proceeding, a few definitions are in order. When we use the term "electronic manuscript," we are referring to everything you have typed and stored on your computer in the process of creating the electronic version of your text. "Everything" includes not only the text you have typed but also any codes you have typed in (generic codes for your publisher, formatting commands for your printer) as well as all the codes that are not visible on the screen or on a printout but that nevertheless are there. By "electronic text," on the other hand, we are referring only to the data in your files, in this case all the words, spaces, and punctuation that will appear in print in the finished book, and not to any of the codes. When we use "electronic medium" or "magnetic medium," we mean the magnetic tape or disks upon which your electronic manuscript is stored. "Electronic files" refer to the organizational units you have created for the purposes of storage and recall while working at the computer; in the case of books, most of you create one file per chapter. (For definitions of "electronic processing" and "conventional processing," see the introduction.)

1.3 In conventional processing, typesetting personnel retype the entire manuscript into the typesetting system. As they are doing so, they often make "silent" corrections, especially with regard to certain common stylistic errors or inconsistencies. Electronic processing lacks the intervention of typesetting personnel in these matters, and so certain points of style take on additional importance. Although simple spelling errors are easy enough to correct, stylistic mistakes can create difficult problems for you, your publisher, and the typesetter. In the hope of steering you away from this second kind of mistake, we provide instructions on some specific points of style (see 1.48–1.57). For more general advice on matters of punctuation, capitalization, italicization, and bibliographic style, you are urged to consult *The Chicago Manual of Style*.

1.4 There are two important points to keep in mind as you read this guide and prepare your manuscript. First, the typesetter will generally reproduce, character for character, the electronic text that is stored on your magnetic tape or disks. (Occasionally, inexplicable machine errors can occur, but these are usually few.) The obvious advantage to electronic processing is that proofreading time can be reduced, but it also carries with it an additional responsibility. It is *crucial* that the magnetic medium supplied contain all editorial revisions and that the electronic text correspond *exactly* to the edited printout. Second, you should not use decorative formatting on your manuscript page. The lure of a word processor's ability to center or embolden chapter titles and subheads is a powerful one, but the final typeset appearance of these elements will be determined later, by the book's designer. The codes that are embedded in your text when you use these word processor features are useful only to your system's printer or screen and usually must be removed from the text before typesetting can begin. Therefore, such formatting should be kept to a minimum. The electronic manuscript supplied to the publisher ideally would consist of a "text stream" of editorially accurate text plus generic codes uninterrupted by a specific word processor's formatting codes. The text can then be formatted to the book's design specifications by the typesetting computer.

1.5   Let's use the handling of block quotations as an example of how traditional typing conventions differ from the requirements for electronic manuscripts. An author typing a manuscript for conventional typesetting sets off a long quotation from the main text by doing the following: dropping down a few lines and indenting from the left and perhaps also the right margin. The copyeditor at some point writes instructions to the typesetter in the margin next to the block quotation on how the material should be handled: The instructions may ask for a reduced type size, less space between lines, an indention from the left margin, and a specific amount of extra space above and below the quote. When the typesetter sees the instructions, he or she types in typesetting codes that produce the requested formatting. In electronic typesetting, however, there is no human being present to read the handwritten marginal instructions at the time the actual processing is done. Instead, the typesetting computer "reads" certain generic codes typed in by the author and converts them to the typesetting codes that are entered manually in conventional typesetting. To be sure, human beings are very much involved in writing the programs that enable the typesetting computer to do the conversions (see introduction). But if the author follows certain rules in typing his or her electronic manuscript, the typesetting computer can do the conversion with a minimum of difficulty. The rules we have found that work for block quotations are the following:

1. Begin typing the block quotation on a new line, flush with the left text margin, with no extra carriage returns (see 1.39) above it.
2. Precede the text of the quotation with a generic code that is used only to flag block quotations.
3. Keep the same spacing for the block quotation that is used for the main text.
4. End the block quotation with an exit code and a single carriage return.
5. Resume typing the main text on the new line, with no additional carriage returns.

The first example that follows shows how long quotations are handled in conventional preparation, and the second example shows the same material as it should be handled for electronic preparation.

Conventional preparation

Distinguishing between a pluralist interest in allocational politics and a welfare-state orientation toward redistributive issues, Greenstone notes that

> organized labor's electoral participation locally . . . reflected a pluralist concern for the organizational interests of particular unions. [In Los Angeles] unions supported a conservative incumbent mayor in 1961 and displayed little enthusiasm for a liberal candidate in 1965.

One explanation for the peculiar conservatism of local trade unions is their small constituency.

Electronic preparation

Distinguishing between a pluralist interest in allocational politics and a welfare-state orientation toward redistributive issues, Greenstone notes that</p>
<bq>organized labor's electoral participation locally . . . reflected a pluralist concern for the organizational interests of particular unions. [In Los Angeles] unions supported a conservative incumbent mayor in 1961 and displayed little enthusiasm for a liberal candidate in 1965.</>
One explanation for the peculiar conservatism of local trade unions is their small constituency.

9

The actual codes that are used in the second example will be explained as we proceed.

1.6   So aside from ensuring legibility, you should not be concerned about the appearance of the resulting printout when you follow this guide. Ignore all the impressive capabilities of your equipment: Abandon your boldface, centered headings, and notes at the bottom of the page. Do not justify (align) your right-hand margins. The line endings in the typeset proofs will be different anyhow, so uneven right-hand margins on your printout are just fine. The manuscript printout is an intermediate stage that allows your publisher to seek readings for the review process and to edit according to house style. The electronic manuscript will be read by another computer; the guidelines presented here are intended to minimize machine incompatibility and allow the electronic transfer to take place more readily.

TYPES OF COMPUTERS

1.7   At this point it might be helpful to describe briefly the four general categories of computers, distinguished primarily by computing power, speed, and memory:

1. dedicated word processors,
2. microcomputers,
3. minicomputers, and
4. mainframe computers.

The distinctions among these categories of computers are not absolute, and they are becoming less and less defined as the technology evolves. For the author, the potentials and limitations of each vary to a large extent with the type of word processing software available and the requirements of the text being produced.

DEDICATED WORD PROCESSORS

1.8   Dedicated word processors are microprocessor-based machines used primarily for producing short, uncomplicated office documents. The keyboard of a dedicated word processor has function keys labeled with common editing operations, such as "copy," "delete," and "insert." They are likely to be found within office environments, where they are used to produce letters, memos, forms, and other paperwork. These systems can be shared ("multiuser") or individual ("stand-alone") units.

MICROCOMPUTERS

1.9   Most microcomputers are single-user, "desktop" machines designed for a variety of computer applications: word processing, programming, data storage and retrieval, and numerical analysis. With a good word processing program, a microcomputer may be nearly as effective as a dedicated word processor in handling many types of documents.

MINICOMPUTERS

1.10   Most minicomputers are fairly powerful multiuser machines designed for a variety of applications. A single minicomputer can often support all the computing needs of a small department in an organization. With appropriate text processing software, minicomputers can manage long, complex documents, elaborate graphics, typesetting, tables, and equations.

MAINFRAME COMPUTERS

1.11   Whereas minicomputers may support the needs of a department, mainframes are sometimes powerful enough to support the needs of an entire organization. Mainframe computers can process large volumes of complex applications, including sophisticated large-scale document production. Mainframes are also very useful for certain types of composition, especially for complex graphics and text merging. In some cases mainframes can be used to overcome incompatibilities between an author's equipment and that of the publisher or typesetter.

PREPARING YOUR MANUSCRIPT FOR SUBMISSION TO A PUBLISHER

1.12   The advice on manuscript preparation offered in sections 1.13–1.87 is directed to authors who are in the first stages of manuscript preparation. When you begin to write a book, you probably will not know whether it will be published, which publisher will accept it, or whether your publisher will want you to submit your manuscript in electronic form. If you follow this guide, your manuscript will be ready for submission to a publisher and will also be properly prepared for later editing and typesetting, either by conventional means or by electronic transfer. If your eventual publisher decides to handle your manuscript conventionally, the generic coding on the printout should not interfere with the typesetter's ability to proceed.

11

1.13 The requirements and capabilities of text editors on mainframe computers sometimes differ from those of dedicated word processors and the word processing software used on microcomputers, as you will see as we proceed.

SOME PRELIMINARIES

1.14 We attempt in this guide to follow the progress of the manuscript from first typing to typeset proofs. However, certain unpleasant surprises later on can be minimized if you are made aware of publishers' requirements at the start. Sections 1.15–1.20 address these requirements. Sections 1.21–1.25 discuss the potential and pitfalls of global search and replace.

Hardware and Software Considerations

1.15 You may select your word processing software and hardware from any number of possible combinations, but the electronic manuscript you eventually supply to a publisher should be prepared on the same system from start to finish. If you are interested in providing a manuscript in electronic form, you should be aware of the following considerations:

1.16 *Mainframe or minicomputer users.* Do not use more than one text editing or formatting program within the same manuscript. If you need to change systems or software, you must transfer your complete text to the new system before submitting the disk or tape to your publisher.

1.17 *Word processor and microcomputer users.* Do not change word processing software or hardware in the middle of your manuscript. For example, do not begin your manuscript using WordStar and switch to WordPerfect later, or prepare some of your manuscript on a Wang system and the rest on a TRS-80. If you find it necessary to change systems or software during the preparation of your manuscript, you must transfer your complete text to the new system.

Input versus Print-ready Files

1.18 Some word processing systems do not automatically position the text for printing as it is being entered. These systems require that the text be entered along with special positioning control words ("format control words"). This text file (the "input file") is then processed, creating a second file ready for printing. When a system of this type is used, the first text file is the one the publisher will generally want for typesetting, not the second, "print-ready" file. Usually the format control words have to be replaced with generic codes. However, testing may determine that all or some of the format control words can be used without replacement.

Printer Considerations

1.19 You should be aware when you are purchasing equipment that many publishers are resistant to the use of dot matrix printers. This resistance is fading somewhat as the quality of dot matrix output improves, but an author who plans to submit the manuscript to a publisher should choose a printer that produces highly readable copy (see 1.94). Just because your dot matrix printer has what the manufacturer calls a "letter quality" mode, do not assume that the use of that mode will ensure an acceptable printout.

File Structure

1.20 Create a new file for every chapter or major subdivision of the text. For example, each chapter, the notes, the bibliography, the tables, the figure legends, and each appendix should be stored in a separate file (see 1.70, 1.76, 1.78, 1.84, and 1.86). Unusually long chapters (more than about eighty double-spaced pages of pica characters) should be divided into two or more files (see 1.118). Copy being moved into additional files should be broken at the end of a paragraph, not in the middle of a sentence or paragraph (see 1.119).

Global Search and Replace

1.21 The global search and replace feature is a powerful and useful tool. The last-minute discovery that you have misspelled the word "twelfth" throughout a manuscript about twelfth-century literature (or, in our case, the word "delimiters" throughout the first draft of this guide) seems not as daunting when one can correct the misspelling quickly. The power available at one's fingertips can be intoxicating and hence admits of a word of caution.

1.22 Because global changes that have not been thought through can create serious and unforeseen problems that cannot be corrected globally, you should exercise great care in carrying out global search and replace. Any spelling, punctuation, and capitalization within quoted material, for example, must remain as it appeared in the original, even if the quotation is then inconsistent with the rest of the text. Thus global changes should ordinarily be made only if the computer or word processor can make such changes on an instance-by-instance basis and if the device shows the context in which the affected word or phrase occurs.

1.23   Remember that both the word to be searched (the "search string") and its replacement (the "replacement string") must be defined precisely. For instance, a global change from roman to arabic numerals would be disastrous if you neglected to include as part of the search string spaces before and after the roman numeral to be changed: the word "approximately" could appear in type as "appro11mately"! Note that on some computer systems defining a word as preceded and followed by spaces will exclude changes of instances of that word located at the beginnings or endings of lines. Consequently procedures for making global changes on such systems will require a few extra steps.

1.24   To illustrate the care that must be taken in making global changes, let's say you wish to change the word "writer" to the word "author" throughout an electronic file. To prevent the unintended changes that would take place if you told your computer to change the string "writer" to the string "author" (for example, to prevent the word "typewriter" from changing to "typeauthor"), you decide to include spaces in the search string:

```
change " writer " to "author"
```

you tell the computer, but you forget to include spaces in the replacement string. The computer obediently follows your instructions, and you end up with "theauthorwas" in place of "the writer was" and so forth. If you try to reverse the damage by asking the computer to

```
change "author" to " author "
```

you may find your manuscript laced with such anomalies as "author ity" instead of "authority" and "author ," and "author ." Thoughtlessly executed global changes really can be irreversible—at least without a lot of extra work and agony. Even when you do define your search string meticulously,

```
change " writer " to " author "
```

there are likely to be occurrences of the word that you want changed that are *not* changed (such as, in this instance, occurrences of the word "writer" that are immediately followed by punctuation) and occurrences of the word that you do not want changed that *are* changed (occurrences of the word within quotations or titles, for example). In other words there may be no single global command that will produce the change you want correctly and completely.

1.25 You must try to anticipate every instance in which the word (technically, the "string") you wish to change occurs in your electronic files before defining your search and replacement strings. Hence our two basic rules for making global changes are (1) think the change through extremely carefully and (2) avoid making the change globally unless you can do it on an instance-by-instance basis and see some of the context each time, enough to determine whether you are within a quote or title. Remember, in addition, to make the global change in each file of your electronic manuscript.

TYPING THE MANUSCRIPT

Els and Ones, Ohs and Zeros

1.26 Never type the letter "el" (l) when you mean the number "one" (1) or vice versa. Do not use the letter to represent the number, as you might with a standard typewriter. Even if the number is not distinguished from the letter on your screen or on your printout, the difference will appear in the typeset proof. Not only do the characters themselves differ, but the space required in type for each character differs: a "one" takes up more space than does an "el." Lest you think this difference may be unimportant or may go unnoticed by readers of the finished book, we provide some examples of what happens when the characters are interchanged:

`little`	prints as	little
`lively`	prints as	lively
`lilliputian`	prints as	lilliputian
`2119`	prints as	2ll9

1.27 One last stern warning: no one has yet discovered an infallible global way of changing els to ones only where they should be changed. This means that if you do not correctly distinguish your els and ones, someone—you, your typist, your editor, or the typesetter—will have to go through the entire manuscript to verify and, if necessary, to correct each occurrence of an el or a one. This is not a task that many people find appealing. So we repeat: do not substitute els for ones!

1.28   For the same reasons, do not interchange "zero" (0), capital "oh" (O), and lowercase "oh" (o).

Spacing

1.29   It may prove helpful to you to develop the habit of leaving two spaces after punctuation that ends sentences (periods, question marks, exclamation points, closing quotation marks at the end of a sentence, etc.) and only one space after colons, semicolons, commas, periods following numbers in lists, and other internal punctuation marks. Such a procedure will allow you to search for the ends (or beginnings) of sentences, or for sentences beginning with a certain word, should the need arise—and it sometimes does. If your publisher requires only one space between sentences, as well as between words, you can, after finishing typing and revising your electronic manuscript, globally change all two-space instances to a single space. Those of you using three blank spaces or three spaces plus a code to indicate the beginning of a paragraph (see 1.35–1.37) will have to protect the three blank spaces from the two-space to one-space global change. To do this, you might temporarily change all occurrences of three consecutive blank spaces to some unused symbol or string, such as three dollar signs ($$$). Then, after the global change of two spaces to one is completed, you would change back the three dollar signs to three blank spaces.

1.30   Since many typesetters seem untroubled by whether you leave one or two spaces between sentences, the Press recommends that its authors leave two. All spacing in your manuscript should be consistent, whether you use two spaces between sentences or one. If you use three blank spaces to indicate paragraph beginnings, or three blank spaces plus a code, use that convention each time a paragraph begins, throughout your electronic manuscript.

1.31   Dashes should be typed as two hyphens, with no space before or after (see 2.100).

1.32   Do not add extra vertical spacing in your electronic manuscript. You should not add extra line spaces above or below chapter titles and subheads, between paragraphs, above or below block quotations, or between footnote and bibliographic entries. The amount of space that will appear around various text elements on the typeset page will be determined by the book designer and will be programmed into the typesetting computer.

1.33 If you need to indicate a text break that will be designated by a line space in the typeset book, use the generic code recommended for special line space, <sp> (see 2.31). Do not use this code above or below chapter titles or subheads, routinely between paragraphs, above or below block quotations, or between footnote or bibliographic entries.

Delimiters

1.34 In 1.33 we mention the generic code for special line space, <sp>. The code consists of some letters, mnemonics in this case since they stand for the word "space," plus angle brackets. The angle brackets are what we call "delimiters," symbols that enable the typesetting computer to distinguish text, which should be printed, from codes, which should not. At the typesetter's, these generic codes will be transformed into specific, usually quite lengthy commands that will tell the system how to print or position something (in this instance, the system will be told to leave a certain amount of extra vertical space before printing the text that follows). The typesetting computer knows not to print the delimiters as well as the characters that occur within them. The Press currently recommends the use of angle brackets as delimiters, except to authors using these symbols frequently as text characters (as "less than" or "greater than" symbols, for example). For more on delimiters, see 2.13–2.17.

Paragraph Beginnings

1.35 Indicate paragraph beginnings in just one of the following three ways:

1. leave three blank spaces followed by the typed-in code for paragraph beginnings, <p>,
2. leave three blank spaces, or
3. use your word processor's special paragraph indent feature, if it has one.

If it is your habit to leave some other number of blank spaces to indicate paragraph beginnings, by all means use that number of spaces. But the number of blank spaces you choose must be at least three, and you must use that exact number of spaces to begin paragraphs throughout your manuscript. If you use three blank spaces, you must use three throughout the manuscript; if you use four, you must use four throughout; and so on. To get blank spaces, you should use the space bar, not the tab key. The first example below illustrates option 1, and the second, option 2. Option 3, using your word processor's paragraph indent feature, would look on the printout like option 2.

```
<p>In the early nineteenth century, geology was a

new, exciting, and fashionable science. It was

experiencing its first and greatest boom in conceptual

innovation, empirical expansion, and public approval

and interest.
```

```
In the early nineteenth century, geology was a new,

exciting, and fashionable science. It was experiencing

its first and greatest boom in conceptual innovation,

empirical expansion, and public approval and interest.
```

1.36 Option 1, using three blank spaces followed by the typed-in paragraph-beginning code, <p>, is much the safest choice and the one least likely to cause problems at the typesetting stage, but it has the disadvantage of requiring additional keystrokes. Option 1 should definitely be your choice if you do not yet have a publisher. If you do have a publisher, your publisher can have the typesetter run a test of a sample disk to determine whether option 2, leaving three or some other given number of blank spaces, is sufficient to indicate paragraph beginnings. Option 3, using your word processor's special paragraph indent key, has never failed to work at the Press, but your publisher should verify its acceptability by having a typesetter test a sample tape or disk. If you do not yet have a publisher, do not use option 3.

1.37 Another consideration affecting your choice of how to indicate the beginnings of paragraphs has to do with whether your electronic manuscript will be sent from one computer to another over the telephone lines (whether it will be "telecommunicated") or whether it will be converted from one magnetic medium to another (disk to tape, tape to disk, one type of disk to another) at some intermediate stage to resolve compatibility problems between your computer and that of your publisher or typesetter. If telecommunications or conversion will be used at some stage (ask your publisher about this), you must use option 1, three blank spaces followed by a generic code, instead of simply leaving three blank spaces. Typed-in paragraph-beginning codes are necessary in these cases because telecommunications and media conversion programs can strip out certain elements from the original electronic manuscript, including extra spaces. When such deletions occur during data transfer, the <p> code saves the day.

Carriage Returns and Wordwrap

1.38 Some word processing software has a feature called "wordwrap" that moves the cursor down a line and all the way to the left whenever the cursor nears the right margin. It does this automatically without your having to hit the carriage return key. Such line breaks can usually be made to occur after full words only and not between words. Wordwrap allows the computer user to type continuously, without hitting the carriage return key until the end of a paragraph. If your machine has an automatic wordwrap feature, use it. Use carriage returns only at the ends of paragraphs, lines of poetry, items in a list, titles, subheads, and block quotations—wherever the end of a line must be maintained in the typeset proof. If your machine does not have automatic wordwrap, see 1.41.

1.39 It should be noted here that the term "carriage return" is a carryover into the computer era of terminology that is only technically accurate with respect to typewriters. Typewriters, of course, really have carriages, and electric typewriters have a key that "returns" the carriage to the left margin and moves the paper up so that typing can begin on a new line. In computer terminology, "carriage return" refers to the key—usually labeled something like "return" or "enter" or picturing an arrow pointing down and then left—that moves the cursor on the computer screen to the left margin and down a line.

Paragraph Endings and Other Forced Line Endings

1.40 Indicate the ends of paragraphs or other line endings that must be maintained in type in one of the following two ways:

1. type in a </p> and then hit the carriage return, or
2. simply hit the carriage return.

The safest choice is option 1, the typed-in code followed by a carriage return. As you will see as we proceed, the end-of-paragraph code, </p>, should not be used at the ends of "display" lines, that is, lines that in the printed version will be distinguished typographically from the main text (titles, subheads, block quotations, etc.). All such display lines should instead end with the exit code </> (see 2.24–2.26).

1.41 If you are using a line editor on a mainframe computer, or word processor or micro that requires hitting the carriage return key at the end of every line, you must use a </p> at the end of every paragraph, line of poetry, item in a list, or other line ending that should be maintained in type (but see 2.26).

1.42 You should also use the </p> (option 1) if your electronic manuscript will be telecommunicated or converted from one medium to another at an intermediate stage. Explicit end-of-paragraph codes are necessary in these cases because one of the elements that may be stripped out by telecommunications and conversion programs is the original machine's carriage return characters.

1.43 Whichever way of indicating paragraph endings you choose, you must use that option uniformly. Never, ever intermix methods. You *must* pick just one end-of-paragraph option and stick to it throughout your manuscript.

```
<p>In our family, there was no clear line between

religion and fly fishing. We lived at the junction of

great trout rivers in western Montana, and our father

was a Presbyterian minister and a fly fisherman who

tied his own flies and taught others. He told us about

Christ's disciples being fishermen, and we were left

to assume, as my brother and I did, that all

first-class fishermen on the Sea of Galilee were fly

fishermen and that John, the favorite, was a dry-fly

fisherman.</p>

The countries participating were</p>

<l>Algeria</p>
```

Angola</p>

Australia</p>

Austria</p>

(For an explanation of the <l> code preceding the word "Algeria," see 2.55.)

Underlining and Italics

1.44   To identify the titles of books and periodicals, foreign terms, and stressed words or phrases that should appear in italic type in the finished publication (see 1.67), use the following methods:

1.45   *Mainframe and minicomputer users.* Alas, the underline commands on many text editing systems do not easily translate into typesetting commands for italics. Instead of the underline command, use the generic codes recommended to begin and end italicized passages, <i> and </i> (see 2.38–2.40).

1.46   *Word processor and microcomputer users.* You may be able to use your word processor's machine commands for underlining to indicate words or phrases that will appear in italic type. In most cases the typesetter will be able to translate your underlining to italics (see 2.7). If the test of the sample disk reveals that the typesetter cannot translate your underlining to italics, you will have to use the typed-in generic codes <i> and </i> recommended in 2.38–2.40.

1.47   Again, if your electronic manuscript will be telecommunicated or converted at some point, the generic codes for italics, <i> and </i>, must be used instead of machine underlining because underlining can be erased during the data transfer.

SOME MATTERS OF STYLE

1.48   The following remarks on style are not specific to authors preparing their manuscripts electronically, but they are more important to them. With conventionally processed manuscripts, the whole text is rekeyboarded by the typesetter, who simply follows the text and the corrections marked on the manuscript. With electronic processing, on the other hand, every change that is indicated, no matter how small it is, represents time that must be spent by someone—usually you, the author—correcting something that already exists. Such matters as whether to place a comma before or after final quotation marks can still be left to the copyeditor, who will indicate any changes on the printout. But authors can save themselves considerable time if they get these details right from the beginning.

Punctuation with Italics and Quotation Marks

1.49 Punctuation marks are usually typeset in the same type style as the letter or symbol immediately preceding them. Hence a period, comma, colon, semicolon, or question mark immediately following a word that will be italicized should be underlined or inserted before the generic code used to indicate the end of the italicized passage (see 2.38–2.40).

1.50 A closing parenthesis or bracket is not italicized unless the opening parenthesis or bracket is italicized.

1.51 Periods and commas should be placed within closing quotation marks:

```
The men had been saved by the master's "coolness,
self-possession, and decision."

See Brighton's comments on "political expedience,"
which may be found in chapter eight of this volume.
```

1.52 A semicolon or colon should be placed outside closing quotation marks:

```
He wondered why she objected to the portrayal of the
"New Woman"; after all, it seemed inoffensive enough
to him.
```

1.53 A question mark or exclamation point should be placed inside closing quotation marks only when it is part of the original quoted material:

```
He called out, "Do you know that thousands are dying
for this?"

Did you hear him say, "McCavity's not there"?

The woman cried, "Those men are beating that child!"
```

```
Her husband replied--calmly--"It is no concern of

mine"!
```

Ellipses

1.54   If you use ellipsis points (three equally spaced dots) to indicate that material has been omitted from a quoted passage, you should use spaces to separate the dots from each other and from the text preceding and following:

```
The gulf . . . widened on two crucial points, around

which polemics between the two camps continued to

revolve until the outbreak of World War II.
```

1.55   If the sense of what is being omitted requires that other punctuation such as the comma precede or follow the ellipses, that other punctuation should be separated from the ellipsis point adjoining it by a space:

```
In this constancy of ineffectuality, virtually of

somnambulism, the real proletariat, if it could be

located . . . , would be an aesthetic relief.
```

1.56   If you wish to include with the ellipses the closing punctuation (period, question mark, exclamation point, colon, or semicolon) of the material quoted, the original punctuation should immediately follow the last word of the sentence. The remaining three dots should be equally spaced from each other and from the text following them:

```
On such nights the stove acquires a special

significance. It is an old cast-iron Franklin with

ill-fitting panels: the fire glows and breathes

through the cracks. . . . Over the table a white glass

lamp casts a cone of bright light on an island of

books, drafts, page proofs, and scribbles.

Why did the <i>Mignonette</i> founder? . . . After

the story broke in England, there was a certain amount
```

of speculation on the matter, and various views were put forward.

(The codes <i> and </i> in the above are the codes for italics; see 2.23–2.25.)

Initials

1.57 Initials in a personal name should be followed by spaces; other abbreviations should be closed up:

T. S. Eliot

J. P. Morgan

U.S.A.

e.g.

i.e.

THE PRINTOUT PAGE

1.58 The layout of your finished book and the type styles for chapter openings, subheads, block quotations, and other elements will be determined by a book designer when your finished manuscript has been accepted for publication. Since these design decisions will not yet have been made when you are preparing the manuscript, you should not attempt to make your manuscript page approximate a typeset page (see 1.4–1.6).

1.59 Your publisher will expect to receive a printout of the manuscript that is double-spaced throughout. Single-spaced copy may be acceptable for the publisher's initial review stage, but the copyeditor must have a double-spaced printout. If you cannot easily change your printer commands from single to double spacing once your text is complete, be sure you produce a double-spaced manuscript from the beginning.

Margins

1.60 The printout you eventually submit for copyediting should have margins of at least one inch on all four sides of the page.

1.61 You should not use a program that justifies your text (makes the right-hand margin even). These programs work by adding extra spaces between words or letters. In some cases such spaces may appear in the typeset proofs, unless the publisher or typesetter removes them—a very time-consuming and expensive process. Remember that copyeditors are accustomed to uneven right margins. Uneven right margins on your printout are perfectly acceptable—indeed, they are preferable (see 1.6)—and will not cause problems for either your copyeditor or your publisher. The margins will be justified by the typesetter.

Line Length

1.62   Because pica type is preferred by many publishers and typesetters, keep your line lengths at sixty-five characters or less. Many publishers' and typesetters' systems have screens that show only eighty characters at a time, and working with lines of text that run off the screen can be difficult, if not impossible. Also, many kinds of printers are not able to print out lines longer than eighty characters. In the event that your publisher may need to produce a printout of your manuscript using such a printer, keeping the lines short will ensure that the publisher is able to do so (see 1.123).

Hyphens and Hyphenation Programs

1.63   If you are using a line editor, do not divide a word at the end of a line or begin or end a line with a hyphen or dash. Such hyphens and dashes (with any end-of-line spaces that may be added automatically by the computer) will appear in the typeset proof, unless you, your publisher, or the typesetter removes them.

1.64   Some software allows you to tell it where given words can be hyphenated should the need arise. Do not insert any of these discretionary hyphens or use hyphenation programs of any kind.

Titles and Subheads

1.65   When typing part titles, chapter titles, or subheads in your manuscript, use what is known as "title capitalization": capitalize all words except articles ("the," "a," "an"), conjunctions ("and," "or," "nor," "but"), and prepositions ("with," "from," "to," "between," etc.) unless such words are the first or last words of the title or subhead. Do not use all capital letters:

```
The Roar of the Crowd
```

not

```
THE ROAR OF THE CROWD
```

1.66 Type titles and subheads flush with the left text margin of your manuscript and label them with the generic codes recommended in 2.24.

1.67 Do not underline part titles, chapter titles, or subheads. Reserve your underline command for those words and phrases within the text that conventionally appear in italic type in the finished publication, such as stressed words and phrases, book and periodical titles, and foreign terms (see 1.44–1.47 and 2.38–2.42).

1.68 Do not use the commands for boldface or centering to identify part titles, chapter titles, subheads, or other parts of your manuscript, because your publisher may later require that you remove these commands from the electronic medium so that typesetting can proceed smoothly.

Running Heads

1.69 Do not add running heads automatically at the top of manuscript pages, because the typesetter must remove the running head text and the printer commands before processing the manuscript. The publisher will provide running head copy for your book according to the publisher's house preferences.

Footnotes

1.70 Do not, under any circumstances, use your machine's ability to position footnotes at the bottom of text pages. All notes should be in a separate file, gathered together at the end of the manuscript (see 1.78–1.83 and 2.64–2.71).

1.71 Some computer systems have facilities for automatically numbering footnotes. These systems generally require that the footnote text either be embedded in the main text, immediately following the command for the text superscript number, or be collected together at the end of the file in which they belong. If you have such a system, you must make provision for publishers like the Press requiring that superscript reference numbers be explicit and that the notes for all chapters be collected together in a file of their own.

Formatting or No Formatting?

1.72 All these exhortations against using the extensive formatting capabilities of your word processing software may be alarming. If you need a formatted copy of your manuscript, by all means make one, but be advised that the final tape or disks you send your publisher for typesetting should have all machine-specific word processing codes deleted, except the following, *all of which are subject to verification by a typesetter's test of a sample magnetic medium:*

1. the underline to identify words or phrases you want to appear in italic type in the finished publication (see 1.44–1.47),
2. the machine superscript for text footnote numbers (see 1.81– 1.82 and 2.93–2.96),
3. the carriage return to indicate paragraph endings and other forced line endings that must be maintained in type (see 1.40– 1.43),
4. machine diacritics (see 2.90–2.92), and
5. your paragraph indent command (see 1.35–1.37).

But the electronic medium supplied to your publisher for editing or typesetting should not contain any commands for boldface, centering, running heads, footnoting, justified margins, or hyphenation. (For pagination, see 1.97.)

MATHEMATICAL TEXT

1.73 Mathematical or statistical text can be extremely difficult to prepare for electronic typesetting (see 2.81–2.87). You may use any of the various software packages that are available for math preparation, but be aware that these packages are rarely compatible with publishers' text editing or typesetting systems.

1.74 The American Mathematical Society distributes a set of guidelines for the preparation of mathematical text, and chapter 13 of *The Chicago Manual of Style* provides instructions for authors and editors of mathematical manuscripts. If you are preparing mathematical text, you may wish to consult the *Chicago Manual* or the AMS guidelines, but we urge you to refrain from doing extensive coding of mathematical text until you are able to consult with a publisher about the publisher's capabilities and requirements.

TABLES

1.75 Tables present special problems for electronic processing. The coding and formatting requirements for typesetting tables electronically are complex and exacting, and many publishers and typesetters have found that adapting the electronic versions supplied by authors can take longer than setting the tables conventionally. Hence, unless the tables are very simple, most publishers will ask that you not supply them in electronic form. You may, of course, prepare the printout of the tables on your computer; the tables should be included with the printout of the manuscript you send to publishers for review and for editing. Once your manuscript has been accepted for publication, your publisher may ask that you delete the tables from the final disks or tape you submit for editing or typesetting.

1.76 Tables should be prepared in a separate file. You can indicate approximate placement of the tables within your text by typing a message such as the following on a separate line *at the end of a paragraph:*

```
<!Table 5.1 about here!>
```

Do not insert such a message in the middle of a paragraph. Notice that messages or comments to the publisher or typesetter not meant to be printed should begin with the open delimiter and an exclamation point and should end with an exclamation point and an end delimiter (see 2.107). As with conventionally produced manuscripts, exact table and figure placement cannot be known until the page proofs are generated.

1.77 Publishers and authors who prepare tables routinely will find that electronic processing of tabular material can be cost-effective and timely once initial standards for preparation are established. If you are interested in submitting tables in electronic form, you should consult with your publisher very early, preferably before you have begun to prepare the final version of your tables.

NOTES

1.78 Whether they are to be footnotes or endnotes in the finished book, notes should be typed in numerical order, consecutively by chapter, in a file of their own.

1.79 Authors whose computers can automatically number notes should see 1.71.

1.80 Notes, whether they are footnotes or endnotes, should be typed paragraph style (the first line of each note paragraph indented, with runover lines flush left). The number of the note should be typed on the same line as the text of the note and should be followed by a period and one space. Do not use superscript commands for the number of the actual note. Each note should end with the code </p> followed by a carriage return or with only a carriage return, whichever you are using as an end-of-paragraph indicator (see 1.70 and 2.64–2.71):

```
<p>3. Norval Morris and Gordon Hawkins, <i>The
Honest Politician's Guide to Crime Control</i>
(Chicago: University of Chicago Press, 1970).</p>
     <p>4. A. W. Brian Simpson, <i>Cannibalism and the
Common Law</i> (Chicago: University of Chicago Press,
1984), 136.</p>
```

1.81 Within the text of the manuscript, you may be able to use the word processor's superscript command to indicate a note reference (see 1.72 and 1.100). Note numbers in the text follow any punctuation marks except the dash and are placed outside a closing parenthesis:

"And don't let's hear another word about it!"[26]

Perhaps even more ironic in this connection is Holgrave's[2]—and Hawthorne's[3]—volte-face on houses.

From this we can infer that collared peccaries (or javelinas)[7] evolved in wet tropical woodlands.

1.82 If your word processing software does not have a superscript command, you must use the generic code <sup> (see 2.93–2.96).

1.83 Notes should be printed out double-spaced, at the end of the text. The requirements for notes submitted with electronic manuscripts are the same as those for manuscripts that will be set conventionally: at the Press, authors who submit manuscripts with notes either single-spaced or at the bottoms of text pages are asked to prepare revised copy.

BIBLIOGRAPHIES

1.84 Bibliographies should be prepared in a file of their own and printed out double-spaced. Even if the final, typeset bibliography may be formatted with runover lines indented (known as "flush and hang" style), bibliographic entries should be typed paragraph style. Each entry should end with the code </p> followed by a carriage return or with only a carriage return. Your printout should look like this:

```
<p>Turabian, Kate. <i>A Manual for Writers.</i>

5th ed. Chicago: University of Chicago Press,

1987.</p>

<p>Whyte, James Boyd. <i>When Words Lose Their

Meaning.</i> Chicago: University of Chicago Press,

1984.</p>
```

even though the typeset entries in the finished book will look like this:

Turabian, Kate. *A Manual for Writers*. 5th ed. Chicago: University of Chicago Press, 1987.
Whyte, James Boyd. *When Words Lose Their Meaning*. Chicago: University of Chicago Press, 1984.

1.85   For a discussion of the 3-em dash (coded <3m>) that is used in place of the author's name when there is more than one work listed by the same author, see 2.97 and 2.101.

FIGURE LEGENDS

1.86   Figure legends should be typed in consecutive order, paragraph style, in a file of their own. Add the code </p> with a carriage return, or a carriage return alone, whichever you are using as an end-of-paragraph tag, at the end of each legend:

```
<p>Fig. 5. New York Central and Hudson River

Railroad. The first electric locomotive on a test run,

1905.</p>
```

Figure legends, like all other parts of the manuscript, should be printed out double-spaced.

1.87   To indicate the approximate placement of figures within your text, type something like the following on a separate line at the end of a paragraph:

```
<!Figure 5.6 here!>
```

(See 2.107.)

PUBLISHING THE ELECTRONIC MANUSCRIPT

1.88   Sections 1.89–1.103 are directed toward authors whose manuscripts have been accepted for publication. We explain how to prepare and submit a printout for copyediting, how the copyediting may best be added to the electronic medium, how authors should prepare and send electronic media to publishers, and, finally, how indexes can be prepared and submitted in electronic form.

1.89   When your manuscript has been accepted for publication, your publisher will determine whether your equipment is compatible with the publisher's in-house text editing equipment or the typesetter's computer system. Your publisher will also inform you about its procedures for electronic processing (various alternatives are discussed in the introduction to this guide).

1.90   Your publisher may ask you to use your computer to add any editorial revisions agreed upon by you and your copyeditor. If this is the case, you should be sure that when you need to revise your electronic manuscript with copyediting changes you will have access to the equipment on which the manuscript was originally prepared.

1.91   Your publisher will tell you when you should submit your electronic medium. If the publisher will be updating your electronic manuscript on an in-house editing system, you will probably need to send the tape or disks with the printout you submit for editing. If you will be updating the electronic manuscript using your equipment, you will submit the tape or disks to your publisher after you have finished adding the editorial changes (see 1.117–1.141).

SENDING THE PRINTOUT TO THE PUBLISHER

1.92   Once you are satisfied that the manuscript is finished and ready for copyediting, print out a clean, double-spaced copy of the final manuscript. Many copyeditors prefer pica to elite typefaces and letter quality to dot matrix printouts. Publishers often ask that you submit both an original printout and a photocopy: the first for the copyeditor, the second for the design and production departments.

1.93 Once you have submitted these copies to the publisher, you must refrain from making additional changes to the electronic medium until the printout is being copyedited. All changes made after the printout has been submitted to the publisher must be approved by the copyeditor. Hence you must either telephone these changes in to the copyeditor, who can insert them on the printout being edited, or keep track of them on your own printout for later transfer onto the copyedited printout when you receive it later for review. When transferring changes, use a different color from previous changes so that the copyeditor can spot and approve them.

1.94 Although a dot matrix printer may be acceptable for the review stage, many publishers prefer that you use a letter quality printer for the printout you provide for editing (see 1.19). Because some dot matrix characters differ from others by as little as a single dot, such copy can be difficult to read and edit. If you do not have a letter quality printer, try to locate one on which you can produce the final manuscript. If you cannot, you should send your publisher a sample of your dot matrix printout, one that includes both numerals and proper names. Your publisher can determine whether your dot matrix printout is acceptable for editing.

1.95 The printout of the manuscript must be double-spaced throughout: all text, block quotations, notes, appendixes, bibliographies, figure legends, and, later, the index should be double-spaced. The copyeditor will need margins of at least one inch on all four sides.

1.96 The parts of the manuscript you submit to the publisher for editing should be arranged in the following order:

>   title page
>   table of contents
>   preliminary matter (dedication, epigraph, preface)
>   all text
>   appendixes
>   notes or footnotes

bibliography
figure legends
tables

1.97   You should use your computer's pagination program to number the pages of the manuscript you submit for editing. However, the pagination commands should be deleted from the electronic files before you submit your tape or disks to the publisher for typesetting (see 3.84).

1.98   Many word processing programs will count words and/or characters. It will be a great time-saver to your publisher if you can provide a total word count at the time you deliver the printout for editing. Character counts are less useful since the coding throws off the normal rules for characters per word.

Generic Coding

1.99   At the time your manuscript is accepted for publication, your publisher will inform you of house preferences regarding generic coding. Most publishers do not *require* authors to undertake complete generic coding of their manuscripts; at the Press, author participation is voluntary. But since the addition of generic coding that identifies text elements can be a straightforward process and since it can contribute to a lower book price, we encourage authors to use generic codes to label the various parts of their manuscripts. Instructions on generic coding are provided in chapter 2 of this guide.

1.100   Before you undertake complete generic coding of your manuscript, ask your publisher to test a sample disk or tape made on the equipment you will use to prepare the final electronic version of the manuscript. Your publisher will then be able to tell you whether any of your machine's formatting codes can be used instead of generic codes (see 3.36–3.37).

1.101   Any generic codes you add should be visible on the printout you submit to your publisher for editing. The publisher will mark additional generic codes on the printout for later insertion by you or will add any additional codes needed using the publisher's in-house text editing system (see 2.23).

Spelling Checkers

1.102   Utilities like spelling checkers will not take the place of good copyeditors, but they can eliminate much tedious correcting of simple typographical errors. If your equipment features a spelling checker, use it before submitting your printout to your publisher for copyediting. If you will be adding the publisher's editing changes to the electronic manuscript, you should run the spelling checker once again before turning in your edited electronic files.

1.103 If you are writing in a specialized field, of course, be sure that you have added to your dictionary any specialized terms you have used.

1.104 If your spelling checker will allow you to add prefixes and suffixes to its dictionary, be sure to add any generic codes (including the delimiters) that occur in your manuscript before running the spelling checker.

EDITING AND PROOFING THE ELECTRONIC MANUSCRIPT

1.105 The final updating of the electronic files may be accomplished by the author, by the publisher, or by the typesetter. Sections 1.106–1.111 are directed to authors who will be using their own equipment to add the publisher's editing; section 1.112 is directed to authors whose electronic manuscripts will be updated by the publisher or typesetter.

Author Adds Copyediting

1.106 When editing is completed, the printout will be returned to you so that you can review the publisher's editorial changes. If the editing has been light, with few queries from the copyeditor, you may be able to answer questions and resolve problems with your copyeditor by telephone. In such cases, you may begin adding the editing and any generic codes marked on the printout by the copyeditor to your electronic medium.

1.107 If the editing has been heavy or the manuscript contains many queries from the copyeditor, your publisher may ask that you return the manuscript to your copyeditor after you have approved the editing and resolved any problems. The copyeditor will review your manuscript and ascertain that all queries have been answered, discrepancies have been resolved, and markings are clear. At this time the manuscript will be returned to you, so that you may begin adding the editorial changes.

1.108 Your publisher will provide you with specific instructions for interpreting the editing marks and for adding the editing to your electronic manuscript.

1.109 Certain elements of your manuscript (half-title page, title page, copyright page, table of contents, statistical appendixes, tables) may be set conventionally by the typesetter. Your publisher may provide you with a list of elements that will be set conventionally and ask that you delete these elements from your disks, or from the electronic files that will be put on ("written to") tape before you submit your electronic manuscript for typesetting.

1.110 After you have entered the editing and any generic codes that you have agreed to add (see chap. 2), have deleted any elements that will be set conventionally, have run the spelling checker, and have backed up all your electronic files on disks or tape (see 3.84), print out two new copies of the manuscript, one for the publisher and one for yourself. You should check the new print-out against the edited script to ensure that the electronic medium supplied for typesetting is editorially accurate. The typeset proofs will generally reproduce your electronic text character for character; thus the time spent checking the new printout should reduce the time necessary for reading galleys or page proofs.

1.111 You will need to return to your publisher the complete edited printout (including any sections that may have been deleted from your electronic files), the new printout, the electronic medium, and any supplementary materials your publisher may require (see 1.117–1.141).

Publisher or Typesetter Adds Copyediting

1.112 If the publisher or the typesetter will be adding the copyediting to the electronic version, you should still have an opportunity to review the edited printout before the changes are made. When you review the edited printout, you will need to approve all editing and answer or clarify all queries and return the copyedited printout to your copyeditor by the date specified. If you have not already sent in the electronic medium, you will need to do so now (see 1.117–1.141). At this time the publisher's in-house specialists or the typesetter can begin making editorial changes to the electronic version.

Late Corrections

1.113 In most cases the publisher and typesetter will regard the edited printout, not the tape or disks, as the master copy of your text. Hence, if the typesetter discovers any differences between the electronic medium and the edited printout, the typesetter will alter the electronic version to correspond with the printout, and you may be charged for these alterations.

1.114 If you are adding the editing and you wish to make last-minute corrections or add new material, you must *first* check that the changes are acceptable to your publisher and *second* add the changes to the edited printout as well as to the tape or disks. For these last-minute changes, choose a bright ink or pencil color different from that used by your copyeditor.

1.115 If the publisher is adding the editing and you wish to make additional changes to your text after you have reviewed the edited printout, you should alert your publisher to your proposed changes before the electronic medium is sent to the typesetter.

1.116 Although electronic processing can offer significant cost savings, alterations in proofs are still handled through traditional correction cycles and are still charged at conventional (i.e., higher) rates. Hence any savings achieved by careful initial preparation of your manuscript can be lost if there are many changes in the typeset proofs. Excessive alterations in proof may be charged against your royalties. We cannot stress enough the need to make all corrections in your manuscript at the time these changes are easy and cheap to make: *before* you submit the electronic medium for typesetting.

SENDING THE ELECTRONIC MEDIUM TO YOUR PUBLISHER

1.117 Sections 1.118–1.126 are directed to authors who will provide their publishers with magnetic tape. Sections 1.127–1.132 are for authors who will provide disks. The instructions in sections 1.133–1.141 apply to all authors submitting electronic media to publishers. Authors should follow the instructions for submitting electronic media regardless of the editorial procedure followed.

Magnetic Tape

1.118 If you have not already done so, create a new file for every chapter or other major subdivision of the manuscript. Each chapter, the notes, the bibliography, the figure legends, and the tables should be in a separate file. Chapters longer than two thousand (single-spaced) lines should be broken into two or more files. Note that files transferred to tape generally should be single-spaced even though printouts delivered to your publisher *must* be double-spaced.

1.119   If you continue an exceptionally long chapter into a second file, the continuation file should begin with a message such as the following, enclosed in angle brackets:

```
<!Chapter 2 continued!>
```

The message should be handled as a nonprinting comment (see 2.107).

1.120   Add an end-of-file generic code to the end of every file. To do this, type the code <eof> as the last line of text in each file. Note that the code letters must be enclosed in angle brackets.

1.121   Add an end-of-book generic code (the code <eob>) to the end of the last file that will be on the tape. Note that the code letters are enclosed in angle brackets.

1.122   The order of files on the tape should correspond to the order of elements in the book; e.g., chapter 2 should follow chapter 1 (see 1.96).

1.123   When making the magnetic tape, be sure that the record length set for the tape is longer than the longest line of your text. This is a crucial consideration, because any characters at the ends of lines that exceed the maximum record length specified may be dropped in the transfer of text from your computer files to the magnetic tape or in the transfer from your tape into the publisher's or typesetter's system. The missing characters will not be noticed until the typeset proofs arrive; it is virtually impossible to reinstate them except by word-for-word proofing of the typeset proofs against the edited printout, followed by typesetting of the dropped characters.

1.124   We recommend that you set a line length for your formatting program of less than sixty-five characters and set a minimum record length for the magnetic tape of eighty characters. In this way the problem of dropped characters may be avoided entirely (see 1.62).

1.125   Your publisher will provide you with recommended specifications for the magnetic tape you supply. You should send your publisher written specifications for the tape you supply, even if it matches your publisher's recommendations exactly. Your written specifications should include the following information:

> number of tracks on the tape
> tape density (800 or 1600 bits per inch)

labeled or unlabeled
code set (standard ASCII, DEC ASCII, or EBCDIC)
parity (odd or even)
record format (fixed or variable, blocked or unblocked)
maximum record length
number of records
maximum block size
number of blocks
blocking factor (records per block)
number of files on the tape

1.126 Once you have written your files to tape, do not delete any on-line files until you are certain that your tape is good (see 1.133).

Disks

1.127 Keep files per chapter to a minimum; usually there is no need for more than one or two files per chapter. If possible, create a new file for every chapter.

1.128 Try not to use more than one disk per chapter. If you find it necessary to continue an exceptionally long chapter on a second disk, begin the continuation file with a nonprinting message like the following:

```
<!Chapter 2 continued!>
```

Remember to split the text that is going on different disks between, not within, paragraphs (see 2.107).

1.129 Chapter files should be in consecutive order on the disks you submit to your publisher: for example, if your manuscript will be submitted on three disks, the first disk should contain chapters 1, 2, and 3, the second disk chapters 4, 5, and 6, and so on (see 1.96).

1.130 If you have prepared other documents on your system and stored them on your disks, be sure to delete these files before submitting your disks to your publisher.

1.131 If you are submitting multiple disks, you should number the disks consecutively using a felt-tip pen.

1.132 If you plan to send (''upload'') your word processor or microcomputer files to a university or corporate mainframe or minicomputer and to supply your publisher with a magnetic tape, you should follow the instructions in 1.118–1.126 for file management and tape preparation.

Safety Tips

1.133 Always make a backup copy of the final version of the disks or tape that you send to your publisher and retain a copy of the printout as well.

1.134 Do not place your tape or disks on metal surfaces, and do not place metal objects like paper clips on magnetic media. Of course, follow all safety tips recommended by the manufacturer of your medium.

1.135 Do not expose your disks or tape to the sort of electronic scanning devices that are commonly used to monitor library exits or to check passengers and their carry-on luggage at airports. Such devices could erase your entire electronic manuscript.

1.136 Your publisher will probably ask you to mail the tape or disks rather than send the electronic manuscript over the telephone lines. In book publishing, the length of most manuscripts makes them poor candidates for long-distance telecommunication, given the present state of the technology. Saving a day or two in delivery time may not be as important as ensuring the safety of your manuscript. Many computer supply stores sell plastic or cardboard cases that are designed specifically for transporting electronic media. We recommend that you use such cases when mailing your tape or disks to your publisher. If mailing cases are not available, the disks should be carefully wrapped, so as to be inflexible. Mark "Do Not X-Ray—Magnetic Media Enclosed" on the outside wrapper of the package.

Supplementary Materials

1.137 If you and your publisher have agreed that some elements of your manuscript will be set conventionally and will not be submitted in electronic form, you should send a list of these elements with the edited printout, new printout, and tape or disks you submit to your publisher.

1.138 Your publisher will need a list of your file names, plus a description of the contents of those files if this is not evident from the file names. Authors submitting multiple disks should indicate on the list of file names which files are on which disk.

1.139 Supply a list of the generic codes you have used in your manuscript and their meanings, whether or not the codes used were recommended by your publisher. The list must include *only* those codes appearing in your manuscript, not codes recommended but never used. This is because typesetting personnel must write a conversion program for each generic code on your list. Writing programs for codes you list but do not use will drive up the typesetting bill.

1.140 If you have changed systems since first informing your publisher about your equipment (see 1.15–1.17), you will need to provide your publisher with detailed information about the system you are using to produce the final version of your manuscript.

1.141 A checklist that may be helpful to you in assembling the electronic manuscript and necessary documentation appears as Appendix C of this guide.

INDEXES

1.142 Information on how to compile an index can be found in chapter 18 of *The Chicago Manual of Style,* available separately in a paperback edition called *Indexes.* The following comments address indexing aids available on some word processing systems and provide instructions for submitting an index in electronic form.

Computerized Indexing

1.143 Many readily available word processing programs offer automatic indexing capabilities—that is, the computer can search for and list key words and indicate the pages in the document or file where these terms occur. But the page numbers of the printout and the electronic file will not correspond to the page numbers of the typeset proofs; thus computerized indexing is less useful in the publishing process than it might seem at first. Several programs offer a feature that helps overcome this problem: once you have the page proofs in hand, you can break the pages in the electronic file into numbered increments that correspond exactly to the pages of the typeset proofs. The index can then be generated from the repaginated files. You will of course want to weigh the time needed to break up a book-length work into page increments against the time needed to prepare the index without the help of the computer.

1.144 Automatic indexing is ideal for compiling straightforward list-ings of place names, titles, or author names. It is less reliable for the more subtle distinctions required of a subject index. You should not rely exclusively on computerized indexing when pre-paring your index. If you plan to prepare your index automati-cally, consult your publisher before doing so.

Preparing and Submitting an Index in Electronic Form

1.145 Sections 1.146–1.150 provide instructions for the final prepara-tion and submission of the index to the publisher. Authors who do not wish to use a computerized indexing capability can never-theless prepare the index on a computer and submit it in elec-tronic form; authors who do use computerized indexing for com-piling the index should also follow these instructions. A properly prepared index submitted in electronic form can be a real boon to everyone: typesetting costs can be reduced, and no one needs to do a word-for-word proofreading of printout against typeset proof.

1.146 Indexes should be prepared very much like bibliographies (see 1.84). They should be typed paragraph style even though the final, typeset index is likely to be formatted in "flush and hang" style. Each entry should end with the code </p> followed by a carriage return or with a carriage return alone, whichever you are using to tag the ends of paragraphs.

```
<p>Doctrine of state action, 306</p>

<p>Douglas, William Orville, 9, 16, 17, 121, 159,

186, 190, 193, 196, 208, 213, 215, 224, 241, 253,

317</p>

<p>Due process clauses: and common law, 24, 25,

28; original meaning of, 24; as outgrowth of natural

rights and social compact doctrines, 24, 26, 34.

<i>See also</i> Economic rights; Fifth Amendment;

Judicial review; Substantive due process</p>
```

The index should be printed out double-spaced.

1.147   The en dash is shorter than a standard dash and longer than a hyphen, and is used in type between inclusive numbers. In the index, en dashes will need to be distinguished from ordinary hyphens. Since the en dash is not available on ordinary keyboards, we suggest that you use the generic code <n> for en dashes between inclusive numbers in the index (see 2.99):

```
144<n>45, 277<n>78
```

which will appear in print as

144–45, 277–78

Leave no space before or after the code.

1.148   Use the generic code for line space, <sp>, between alphabetical sections of the index (see 1.33 and 2.31). The code should be typed flush with the left text margin, on a line by itself, and should be enclosed in angle brackets:

```
<p>ITT, 178</p>
<sp>
<p>Jamaica, 122, 125, 206<n>8, 215<n>23, 250,
276, 289<n>93, 300<n>310, 312, 319, 343,
368<n>70</p>
<p>Jasper, 247, 268</p>
```

1.149   Under no circumstances should you type your index flush and hang (see 1.84) or double-column. The typesetting computer will take care of these details of formatting.

1.150   You should submit both a printout and the electronic version of your index to your publisher. If the system used to prepare the index is different from the one used to prepare the original text, you should provide your publisher with complete information about the hardware and software used to prepare the index.

2 Generic Coding of Electronic Manuscripts

2.1 In chapter 1 of this guide we refer several times to "generic coding"—the labeling of chapter titles, subheads, block quotations, italicized words, special characters, and so on, with identifying tags, so that the typesetter of the book need not conduct a word-by-word search through the manuscript to locate and identify such components. In chapter 2 we further explain generic coding, provide instructions for the person entering the coding, suggest appropriate codes to use, and present examples of a manuscript that has been conventionally typed, typed with generic codes, and set in type electronically (see samples A, B, and C at the end of this chapter). Coding may be entered by the author, the author's typist, or the publisher; we assume that the author or typist will enter most of the coding.

STANDARDIZATION EFFORTS

2.2 There are several ongoing efforts to standardize generic coding, so that authors, publishers, and typesetters will use the same set of codes, much the same way as authors, publishers, and typesetters now use standardized proofreaders' marks. Foremost among these efforts, and the one of most interest to authors and publishers, is the Association of American Publishers' Electronic Manuscript Project. The project involves a survey and analysis of the procedures of authors, publishers, typesetters, computer specialists, and librarians. Among its goals is to develop, test, and publish a set of generic codes that will identify all possible text elements and special characters for a variety of purposes.

2.3 While the AAP's Electronic Manuscript Project is in progress, many publishers and typesetters who have chosen to work with electronic manuscripts have developed their own lists of codes. The codes recommended in this guide are those currently in use at the University of Chicago Press: some have been devised by Press staff, some by typesetting vendors, some by enterprising authors, and some by other interested parties. They may differ from codes recommended by other publishers or those recommended by industry groups. We counsel you to check with your publisher for specific guidance on the codes you should use. No matter which set of codes you use, the key to success is to use the codes consistently.

CODING

2.4   The first requirements that must be met in developing a set of codes are that the codes be unique and that they be used uniformly. The requirement of uniqueness can generally be met by enclosing the code characters (usually letters) in a set of delimiters (see 1.34 and 2.13–2.17). The computer is programmed to recognize that characters within these delimiters are identifiers rather than text. Given the two basic requirements, two other important considerations in setting up generic codes are that the codes require very few keystrokes and that they fit nicely within a logical scheme. For instance, all Greek characters could begin with a semicolon followed by a lowercase ''g'' and then a single letter standing for the Greek letter wanted. In one coding scheme, then, a Greek alpha, α, is coded

;ga

A Greek beta, β, is coded

;gb

and so on. In this scheme, the codes are always three characters long. Because of this, the computer needs no final delimiter and one keystroke is eliminated. Unfortunately, trying to keep keystrokes to a minimum often results in codes that are difficult to remember as well as disruptive to someone trying to read a text interspersed with them. Therefore, some coders have tried to devise codes that are easy to remember and that a reader will not mistake for typographic errors or computer ''garbage'' but in doing so have paid a price in keystrokes. With this in mind, one might (as the Press did) decide to code a Greek alpha as follows:

```
<alpha>
```

Such a code is easy to remember and is fairly easily recognized as a code, but it is longer. What the Press has tried to do is compromise between the priority of minimal keystrokes and that of codes easy to remember and easier to read. Sometimes we lean in favor of the longer, easier-to-remember codes. We try to use mnemonics as often as possible, but mnemonics is less and less effective as the code list gets longer and longer. Those actually entering the codes should feel free to commit long or frequently used codes to programmable keys, to write "macros" to handle these codes (a macro is a series of instructions or keystrokes executed by an abbreviated command), to utilize the software's ability to establish short abbreviations for long character strings, or to use short, temporary codes that will later be changed globally to the codes the publisher recommends (see 2.18–2.19).

2.5   Elsewhere we urge both authors and publishers to read this guide from cover to cover rather than simply consulting it as a reference work. We again urge a thorough reading and offer the enticement that those of you willing to read it more closely may be rewarded by discovering that you can get by with less actual coding than at a quick glance might seem necessary. In the coding instructions that follow we cover both the case in which the typesetter *can* use much of the uncoded manuscript and the case in which either the typesetter is not known at the time you begin typing or the typesetter simply *cannot* use the machine codes. We list the fully coded option first because it is much the safer option. Its drawback, of course, is that it requires more work.

2.6   The typeface of the book and the style of type used to identify each element in the book (italic, boldface, small capitals) will be chosen by the book designer as part of the publication process. Generic codes are simply identification tags that can be used to transform text to any typeface, type style, or page format.

2.7   Many typesetting computers can now recognize common word processing codes, such as carriage returns, underlining, and superscripts. When they can, the need for some generic coding is eliminated. Your publisher can determine whether any of these special codes are usable by testing a sample disk or tape. You should consult with your publisher about this possibility before undertaking complete generic coding of the manuscript, especially if you are using uncommon hardware or software (see 3.36–3.37 and 3.39).

2.8   If you do not yet have a publisher, you should take a cautious approach and do the following:

1. use three spaces followed by the code <p> instead of just three spaces to indicate paragraph beginnings,
2. use the code </p> followed by a carriage return rather than a carriage return alone to indicate paragraph endings,
3. use the generic code <sup> instead of your word processor's superscript key to indicate superscript footnote numbers (see 2.93–2.96),
4. unless you have a very commonly used combination of hardware and software, use the generic codes for begin and end italics (<i> and </i>) instead of using underlining, and
5. use the recommended codes for diacritics and other special characters even if your machine has an extended character set that allows you to display and print out these characters (see 2.76–2.92).

2.9   You may develop codes of your own or use codes recommended by other sources if you wish. However, keep in mind the two requirements for any coding scheme you adopt: (1) the codes must be *unique,* that is, they must not occur anywhere in your manuscript as text or symbols, and (2) the codes must be applied *uniformly,* that is, one code must be used to identify one type of text element and must be used every time that element occurs.

2.10   Sometimes you will need to develop codes in addition to the ones recommended in this guide because you are using symbols or structural elements not covered herein. Create your own "user-defined" codes by typing a U. (a capital "ewe" followed by a period) and your own code, and enclose the whole thing in delimiters. For instance, should you find you need an infinity symbol, you might devise the code

```
<U.inf>
```

which you would type into your electronic manuscript every time you wanted an ∞. All codes you devise must, of course, be added to the list of codes you send to your publisher with the printout for editing.

2.11 Type all the generic codes in lowercase letters except the following: (1) the "U." preceding user-defined codes and (2) the codes for capital Greek letters (see 2.83).

2.12 Incorrect spacing around codes can necessitate costly alterations by the typesetter. The general rule is: do not leave space before, within, or after a code unless you want that space to appear in the final typeset version of your book.

DELIMITERS

2.13 Since generic codes are identification labels and should not appear in print, any letters used as codes must be separated from the manuscript text in some way. The code letters should be enclosed in "delimiters"—a pair of characters used only to identify the beginning and end of a code (see 1.34 and 1.4).

2.14 The current industry preference for delimiters is angle brackets: < >. If you do not have angle brackets on your keyboard or if you will need to reserve angle brackets for their conventional meaning of "less than" and "greater than," you can use braces: { } or square brackets: [ ]. Other delimiters may be used, chosen in consultation with your publisher. However, any character that occurs more than occasionally in text should not be used as a delimiter. Occasional instances may themselves be coded (see 2.103–2.105).

2.15 Whatever delimiters you choose, it is crucial that you *not* use these symbols in the text except as delimiters. For example, if you use angle brackets as delimiters, you should not also use them to mean "less than" and "greater than." If you need these symbols in your manuscript, you may code them <gt> ("greater than") and <lt> ("less than"—with an "el," not a "one").

2.16 The same character (or characters) may not be used to indicate both the beginning and the end of the code (e.g., //h1// or $h1$ is not acceptable).

2.17 The delimiters chosen should be used consistently throughout your manuscript. You should select one set of symbols to be used as delimiters and use them every time you use a code. It is not permissible, for example, to use square brackets some of the time and angle brackets at other times. Nor is it acceptable to change delimiters from chapter to chapter or from file to file. Whatever delimiters are used must be used uniformly throughout the manuscript.

FREQUENTLY USED CODES

2.18 If your word processing software allows you to assign abbreviations or commit programmable keys to given character strings, you might like to make your work easier by utilizing this capacity for the most frequently used or difficult to type generic codes. For instance, if the Greek letter epsilon, ϵ, appears regularly in your text, you might assign the code for this letter, <epsilon>, to programmable key 4. In this way you can alleviate some of the burden of coding and reduce typographic errors in the codes as well.

Using Single Symbols as Codes

2.19 Another way of reducing keystrokes and typographic errors in codes would be to use in place of the longer code some symbol available on your keyboard that is not used as a text character (for example, @, #, ¢, or +) and later to make a global change of that symbol to the longer code. Let's say that you have decided to use the </p> generic code followed by a carriage return to denote the ends of paragraphs (see 1.40–1.43). Since this is a code that will occur frequently, you might, as a means of saving yourself keystrokes, decide temporarily to use the symbol @ in place of the </p>. If you do this, you must remember to change the @ to </p> globally in each electronic file before generating your printout and sending it to your publisher for editing.

2.20 One of the problems with using single symbols as permanent codes (or with using single symbols like @ at all) is that whenever an electronic manuscript created on one system is going to another system—say, from your microcomputer to your institution's mainframe or even from your microcomputer to a typesetter's system—there is a chance that that symbol has been defined by a programmer of the receiving system as something like "kill this line" or "kill this character." Programmers of operating systems need to assign such functions to certain characters, and they naturally look for single, rarely used symbols.

TYPES OF CODES

2.21   The codes we recommend are of two types: *identification codes,* which identify parts of the book such as chapter openings and subheads as well as words or passages that should be distinguished typographically from the main text (with italics, for instance); and *special character codes,* which mark those characters or symbols that are not commonly available on computer keyboards or that require special treatment (diacritical marks, superscripts).

IDENTIFICATION CODES

2.22   These codes identify parts of the text, group the text into paragraphs, and specify the kind of type to use: roman or italic. In general, you should identify the beginning and end of any text element that will differ in type from the main text.

2.23   Although some publishers may prefer that the codes be added after editing, the Press as a rule asks its authors to add the identification codes to their electronic manuscripts as they prepare their final drafts so that the codes will be visible on the printout submitted to us for editing. Any additional codes that may be needed are indicated in longhand on the edited printout for insertion by authors at the same time they add the editing to the disks or tape.

2.24   Recommended identification codes:

Code	Exit Code	Element
\<cn\>	\</\>	Chapter number
\<ct\>	\</\>	Chapter title
\<ca\>	\</\>	Chapter author (for multiauthor works only)
\<h1\>	\</\>	First-level subhead, A head (with a "one," not an "el")
\<h2\>	\</\>	Second-level subhead, B head
\<h3\>	\</\>	Third-level subhead, C head
\<nth1\>	\</\>	First-level subhead within the notes section (with a "one")
\<bq\>	\</\>	Block quotation, extract
\<ep\>	\</\>	Epigraph
\<po\>	\</\>	Poetry extract
\<l\>	\</\>	Unnumbered list (with an "el")

Code	Exit Code	Element
\<nl\>	\</\>	Numbered list (with an "el")
\<lh\>	\</\>	List headline (with an "el")
\<eq\>	\</eq\>	Equation
\<i\>	\</i\>	Italics
\<p\>	\</p\>	Paragraph (begin-paragraph code \<p\> to be used following three blank spaces; end-paragraph code \</p\> to be followed by a carriage return)
\<sp\>	None	Special line space

2.25 A complete list of codes appears as Appendix D of this guide.

2.26 There is an important difference between the end-of-paragraph code \</p\> and the exit code \</\>. The \</p\> is used at the end of all regular text paragraphs. It tells the typesetting computer, among other things, to return to the left margin and to continue in the same type style. The \</\> code, on the other hand, identifies the end of an element that will differ in type style from the main text. It signifies not only a return to the left margin but also a shift back into "default," that is, into the type style of the text. The code \</\> preempts the code \</p\>, so you should not use the code \</p\> at the ends of lines that take the code \</\>. In the case of one "display" line immediately followed by another (see 1.40), such as

```
<hl>The Triple Crown Races</>

<h2>The Kentucky Derby</>

   <p>The most prestigious of the races for

three-year-olds is surely the Kentucky

Derby. . . .</p>
```

the first \</\> returns the typesetter to default. But before any text can be printed, a new identification code, \<h2\>, is encountered that sends the typesetter into the type style that has been chosen for second-level heads.

Chapter Openings

2.27 Chapter openings usually contain two elements: a number and title. These are very often treated differently in type (usually a large ornamental numeral is chosen for the chapter number). Hence the number and title should be coded as two different elements:

```
<cn>Chapter One</>

<ct>Happy People Do Not Have a History</>
```

Both the chapter number and the chapter title should be typed flush with the left text margin, in upper- and lowercase letters (not in all capitals). Note that we have used exit codes, but not </p> codes, at the end of each of the elements. In the example above, we have chosen to spell out the chapter number. If you prefer, you may use arabic numerals. Whichever course you adopt, use it consistently throughout your manuscript.

Text

2.28   The main text of your book can be considered the default type style and does not need to be specially coded. Individual paragraphs should begin with three blank spaces followed immediately by the code <p>, or simply with three spaces, whichever you are using to tag the beginnings of paragraphs (see 1.35–1.37).

2.29   If your system does not have an automatic wordwrap feature (see 1.38), you must end each paragraph with the code </p> and a carriage return. If your system does have automatic wordwrap, read sections 1.40–1.43 before making your decision to indicate paragraph endings with (1) a </p> followed by a carriage return or (2) a carriage return alone.

2.30   You should not use your machine's commands for centering or boldface, or type any text element in all capitals (see 1.65–1.68), except for acronyms or other material that must appear in capitals in the printed version.

2.31   If you wish to use a line space to indicate a break in your text (the kind of break that might otherwise be indicated by a subhead), use the code recommended for line space, <sp>, typed flush left on a line by itself. Add a </p> followed by a carriage return (or a carriage return alone) at the end of the text that immediately precedes the line space:

```
The text ends here.</p>

<sp>

Then the text resumes here.
```

The code <sp> is not to be used immediately above or below chapter numbers, chapter titles, or subheads. The spacing requirements of titles and subheads are taken care of by the generic codes assigned to those elements. One legitimate use of the <sp> code would be to get a little extra vertical space to show a break in structure in the main body of the text that is *not* indicated by a subhead or title. Such a text break should be used sparingly, if at all, because if it happens to occur between pages, it will be invisible to the reader. Other appropriate uses of the <sp> code would be to get a little extra space between poetic stanzas and between alphabetic sections of an index (see 1.33 and 1.148).

Different Kinds of Text

2.32   Certain books may contain not one, but several different kinds of text. Some social science books, for example, feature main text, transcriptions of field notes, oral histories, or commentaries. When a manuscript contains different kinds of text, each of which will be treated differently in type, each individual kind of text should be identified with codes. As with other text elements, the main text would not be coded, but the beginning and end of different kinds of text should be identified.

2.33   You will need to examine your text carefully to determine whether there are several different kinds of text rather than simply one default text type. (If your manuscript has been accepted for publication, your publisher can be helpful in determining this.)

2.34   You may use mnemonic codes to label the different kinds of text (for example, <U.tr> for translations, <U.com> for commentary). Be careful not to use the same code twice, as could happen if you need to devise many of these (for example, the use of <U.int> to signal both introductory material and interviews). The "U." indicates that the code is "user-defined" (see 2.9–2.10). An alternative coding scheme is to assign each variant text type a number, as in the following:

<U.tx1>

<U.tx2>

<U.tx3>

Whichever scheme you adopt, you must end each alternative text passage with the exit code </>, which tells the typesetting computer to go back to the main type style.

2.35 In the example below, the text coded <U.int> is introductory material that must be distinguished typographically from the main text, which begins with the words "The *Jazz Singer*":

```
<ct>A Soldier Falls (1929)</>

<ca>Fitzhugh Green</>

<U.int>The most romantic history of the coming of
sound was Fitzhugh Green's <i>The Film Finds Its
Tongue.</i> . . . This chapter from the book
describes the death of . . . Sam Warner, just prior to
the premi<gv>ere of the film that would make the
Warners' name and fame.</>

    <p>The <i>Jazz Singer,</i> starring Al Jolson,
was finished as a Talkie at the Warners' Hollywood
studio in the summer of 1927. The last "take" had been
made on August 7th. . . .</p>
```

In the final book the introductory material, by the editor/compiler of the whole volume, might be distinguished from the text that follows it, by Fitzhugh Green, in any number of ways: it might have reduced spacing between lines and a "ragged" (uneven) right margin, to contrast with the justified (even) margins of the main text.

Front and Back Matter

2.36 Sections like the preface, introduction (if it is not chapter 1), and an appendix may be handled differently typographically from the chapters of a book. The following shows how to code a preface:

```
<pfd>Preface</>

<pftx>Elementary and general accounts of the
invertebrates, suitable for the beginning college
```

```
student or layman, have been limited to two sorts of

books: natural histories, which describe the habits of

a great many animals but are lacking in descriptions

of basic structure and in theory, and formal

textbooks, which are packed with morphological detail

and technical terminology.</>
```

The word ''Preface'' (the preface ''display'' title, in typesetting terminology) must be preceded with the code <pfd> and followed with the exit code </>. The preface text is preceded with the code <pftx> (for ''preface text''). This is because the design for the preface may call for a different type style from that for the main text, which is the default style and should not be specially coded (see 2.28). Since the preface text begins with a code, it must end with the exit code </>, which returns the typesetting computer to the default text style. If the type style the designer chooses for the preface turns out to be identical to that chosen for the main text, the typesetter should be able to proceed without difficulty. Appendix D suggests codes for other front and back matter sections.

2.37 The ''display'' title for an endnotes section (the word ''Notes,'' which is printed at the beginning of the endnotes section) should be coded as follows:

```
<ntd>Notes</>
```

(the <ntd> stands for ''notes display''). The display title for the bibliography or reference list should be handled as follows:

```
<bibd>Bibliography</>
```

(the <bibd> stands for ''bibliography display''). For more on footnotes, see 1.70–1.71, 1.78–1.83, and 2.64–2.71; on bibliographies, see 1.84 and 2.72–2.74.

Italics

2.38 The generic code for begin italics is <i> and for end italics </i>. You should use the generic codes rather than your machine's underlining command in these cases:

1. if your publisher's typesetter determines that your underlining command cannot be translated to italics,
2. if you know your electronic manuscript will be sent from one computer to another by telephone or that it will be converted from disk to tape, tape to disk, or one type of disk to another at some intermediate stage to resolve compatibility problems between your computer, the publisher's system, and that of the typesetter, or
3. if you do not yet have a publisher and you are using hardware and/or software that is new or not in wide use.

If you are not sure whether you fit into category 3, the safest course is to use the generic codes for italics rather than your machine's underlining command. However, if you decide to take a chance that your machine's underline will be usable by the eventual typesetter, you must be prepared to convert all the underlines to generic codes if the typesetter's verdict turns out to be negative.

2.39 You should code for italics only text that is conventionally set in italics, such as stressed words and phrases, the titles of books and periodicals, and foreign words and phrases. Never code complete subheads for italics. If the book designer later on chooses italics as the style for one level of subhead, the subhead codes will take care of the italicization. Within subheads, however, individual words should be coded for italics if they are italicized elsewhere in the text.

2.40 Should you need to switch back and forth between roman and italic type frequently (for instance, if yours is a long bibliographic or reference work), you might find it helpful to set up two of your programmable keys for the italic codes or otherwise utilize your machine's ability to assign abbreviations to designated character strings. You might, on the other hand, use the machine's global change feature (for instance, use { for <i> and use } for </i>), but do not forget to make the global change once per file before generating the printout(s) you will turn in to your publisher for editing.

2.41 Whichever method of tagging italics you choose—underlining or using generic codes—you must not intermix methods. It is not even permissible to use underlining in one file and generic codes in the next. And the same is true for all the codes. Not only must the codes be unique, but also they must be used uniformly throughout your electronic manuscript.

2.42 Punctuation marks are generally typeset in the same style as the letter or symbol immediately preceding them. Hence a period, comma, semicolon, question mark, or exclamation point immediately following an italicized word should precede the code that signals the end of the italicized passage:

```
<i>The Chicago Manual of Style,</i> 13th ed.

The weasel, <i>Mustela,</i> had an efficiency of

26.8 compared with an efficiency of 1.1 for the

herbiferous <i>Microtus pennsylvanicus.</i>
```

A closing parenthesis or bracket should not be italicized unless the opening parenthesis or bracket is italicized.

Other Emphasized Text

2.43 Italics is the conventional way of distinguishing some text from the main roman text, particularly stressed words and phrases, book and periodical titles, and foreign terms. But it is not the only way of emphasizing text. If you or your publisher wishes to resort to other typographic strategies for emphasizing text, such as using boldface, small capital letters, or even color shading, you will need to use different codes for each type of emphasized text. Let's say you have in mind using italics for stressed words, titles, and foreign terms, and you know you want to distinguish important definitions and glossary terms but are not sure at the time of typing the manuscript exactly what the final typographic decisions will be. Whether you know these decisions or not, you can use "emphasis codes," <e1> and </e1> (with a "one," not an "el"), <e2> and </e2>, and so on. The choice of what the emphasis codes stand for (say, <e1> and </e1> for begin and end boldface, and <e2> and </e2> for begin and end small capital letters) can be made much later, by you and your publisher. The codes are generic, so they can be defined to stand for whatever you and your publisher decide they should stand for.

```
The <i>Textbook for Astronomy</i> reports that, in

addition to dust, the material in the
```

```
<el>interstellar medium</el> consists of cold, dense

clouds with radii of a few parsecs and clouds of

neutral hydrogen, both immersed in a hot, dilute

<el>intercloud medium.</el>
```

2.44   Do *not* use your machine's boldfacing (overstriking) command at any time. The boldfacing command is much less likely than the underlining command to be usable by your publisher's or the typesetter's computer system.

Subheads

2.45   Subheads (<h1> for first-level heads, <h2> for second-level heads, <h3> for third-level heads) should be distinguished by codes alone, not by decorative formatting. They should be typed flush with the left text margin in capital and lowercase letters, title style. They should not be centered, typed in all caps, or underlined. They should not end with periods. The text preceding the subhead should end with a </p> followed by a carriage return or with a carriage return alone. No extra space should be left above or below the heading. The subhead itself should end with the exit code </>, followed by a carriage return:

```
When Brendan learned how to use Superwylbur, he knew

his life would never be the same.</p>

<h1>The End of Cut and Paste</>

    <p>He had discovered the advantages of word

processing while writing his doctoral dissertation

. . .</p>

<h2>Conventional Pagination Procedures</>

    <p>Before the advent of electronic pagination

. . .</p>
```

Block Quotations, or Extracts

2.46   Most quotations are short enough that they can be run into the text and enclosed in quotation marks. Longer quotations, those of one hundred or more words or more than about eight typewritten lines, are often set off from the text as block quotations (sometimes called "extracts"). In typeset material these blocks may be indented from the left margin, indented from the left and right margins, set in a slightly smaller type size, set with reduced space between the lines of type, and/or preceded and followed by some extra vertical space (see 1.5 and 2.71).

2.47 Like subheads, block quotations should be distinguished by codes alone and should not be indented from the margin or single-spaced. A </p>, or carriage return alone, whichever you are using as an end-of-paragraph tag, should be typed at the end of the text that immediately precedes the block quotation. The block quotation itself should begin on a new line and should be labeled with the generic code <bq>. The first line of the block quotation should not begin with a paragraph indent code, and the body of the block quotation should be typed flush with the left text margin. The block quotation should end with a </> code. No extra space should be left above or below the block quotation. (The examples given here illustrate coding only and are purposely shorter than a block quotation would normally be.)

```
We are introduced to Emma's way of thinking in the way

she is described in the opening sentence:</p>

<bq>Emma Woodhouse, handsome, clever, and rich, with

a comfortable home and a happy disposition, seemed to

unite some of the blessings of existence; and had

lived nearly twenty—one years in the world with very

little to distress or vex her.</>
```

2.48 Block quotations of more than one paragraph from the same source should begin with the code <bq>. The first paragraph should immediately follow the code (no begin-paragraph code); the second and subsequent paragraphs should start with begin-paragraph codes. There should be a </p>, or carriage return alone, at the end of each paragraph except the last, and an exit code (</>) at the end of the last paragraph of the quoted passage. No extra space should be left between the paragraphs of the quotation.

```
<bq>It is impossible to overemphasize the importance

of meticulous accuracy in quoting from the works of
```

others. Authors should check every direct quotation against the original if possible or against a first, careful transcription of the passage.

    Checking quotations is an operation to be performed on the final typescript, not left until type has been set.</>

2.49   Block quotations of material from two or more different sources should be handled somewhat differently from multiparagraph quotations from the same source. The first excerpt should immediately follow the code <bq>. Subsequent excerpts should begin flush left on a new line, with no code. All excerpts except the last should end with a </p> or a carriage return alone. The last excerpt should end with the exit code, </>. Between each excerpt, flush left on a line by itself, should be typed the code for a line space, <sp>.

The calendar to which this sect adhered is mentioned in <i>The Book of Jubilees</i> and <i>The Book of Enoch:</i></p>

<bq>And all the days of the commandment will be two and fifty weeks of days, and these will make the entire year complete . . . And command thou the children of Israel that they observe the years according to this reckoning—three hundred and sixty-four days, and these will constitute a complete year.<sup>2<sup>7

<sp>

And the sun and the stars bring in all the years exactly, so that they do not advance or delay their position by a single day unto eternity; but complete the years with perfect justice in 364 days.<sup>2<sup>8</>

> This calendar was quite distinct from the one adhered
>
> to by the Jewish community at large around that time.

2.50 Whether the block quotation is one paragraph or more, the text following it should begin on a new line, as illustrated in the example above. If the text is a continuation of the paragraph that precedes the quotation, it should not start with a begin-paragraph code; if the text is a new paragraph rather than a continuation of the preceding paragraph, it *should* start with a begin-paragraph code.

Poetry

2.51 Poetry extracts should be handled in much the same way as prose extracts. The beginning of the poem should be identified with the code <po>. Each poetic line should begin on a new line and should end with the code </p> or a carriage return alone, whichever you are using as an end-of-paragraph tag. The last line of the poem should end with an exit code (</>).

```
<po>I grip these gifts which only look

like stars</p>

And draw vague lines across uncrafted seas,</p>

And map by these.</>
```

2.52 To indicate a stanza break, use the code for line space (<sp>), typed flush left on a line by itself:

```
<po>But now they laugh in the dark.</p>

Lighting her cigarette,</p>

<sp>

Marcel makes a world around them,</p>

A short, shining world.</>
```

2.53 Poetic lines too long to fit on one line of the screen or the print-out should be allowed to wordwrap to the next line:

```
<po>Perhaps they are sampling the fresh dew that

gathers slowly</p>

In empty snail shells</p>
```

```
And in the secret shelters of sparrow feathers fallen

on the earth.</>
```

2.54   The variable indents that often occur in dramatic verse and poetry (especially contemporary poetry) need special coding. What
is wanted in such text is a certain alignment of the beginning of
one line with respect to words on the line above or below it.
Using the space bar is not sufficient in these cases, because many
typesetting systems are designed to "see" multiple spaces as a
single space, and using a tab key is not recommended. What is
needed is a code that will tell the typesetting computer to leave
a space equal to certain text but not to print that text. We have
established the codes <xp> for "stop printing but leave space"
and </xp> for "resume printing." Within the codes should be
typed the text above or below the line that equals the desired
indent of the line being typed. The text within the codes will be
used to position the current line but will not itself be printed.
For instance, to get the following result in your printed book:

and the eye that sees them refuses
to see further, glances off the
surfaces that
            speak and conjure,
rests
      on the frail
      strawness of straw, metal sheen of tinsel,

you should type the following:

```
<po>and the eye that sees them refuses</p>

to see further, glances off the </p>

surfaces that</p>

<xp>surfaces </xp>speak and conjure,</p>

rests</p>

<xp>rests</xp>on the frail</p>

<xp>rests</xp>strawness of straw, metal sheen of

tinsel,</>
```

Notice that in line 4 of the coded version the space following
the word "surfaces" in line 3 is included between the codes

<xp> and </xp>. If the space were not included between the codes, the word "speak" in line 4 would not line up directly under the word "that" of line 3. As you can see, coding such material requires many additional keystrokes, but so far this seems to be the only way to produce the exact indents that are sometimes required not only in poetry and drama, but also in other material as well.

Lists

2.55   *Unnumbered lists* should be handled in much the same way as poetry extracts, except that the generic code beginning the list should be <l> (note that this is an "el" for "list," not a "one").

```
The ingredients Ann needed for her famous pumpkin pie

included the following:</p>

<l>pumpkin</p>

milk</p>

brown sugar</p>

eggs</p>

cinnamon</>

The pie won a contest sponsored by a Hartford

newspaper.
```

2.56   *Numbered lists of fewer than ten items* should be handled as follows:

```
The largest breeds in the world are the

following:</p>

<nl>1. Irish Wolfhound</p>

2. Russian Wolfhound</p>

3. Mastiff</p>

4. Saint Bernard</p>

5. Great Dane</>

Each breed has its own special attributes, but the
```

```
Great Dane was John's personal favorite, both in looks

and in personality.
```

The <nl> (with an "el") stands for "numbered list."

2.57   In *numbered lists of ten or more items* a space code must be inserted in front of each of the single-digit numbers so that the periods following the numbers will align vertically:

```
The states Katie visited on her summer vacation

were</p>

<nl><ns>1. Indiana</p>

<ns>2. Ohio</p>

<ns>3. Pennsylvania</p> . . .

10. Connecticut</p>

11. New Hampshire</p>

12. Maine</>

She did not consider her trip complete until . . .
```

The <ns> code stands for "en space" and needs no exit code. It is a special character or symbol code like those discussed in 2.76–2.105 and is typed in place of what is wanted in the text.

2.58   If you have a computer that will number lists automatically, you must make provision for publishers such as the Press that require explicit numbers.

Equations and Tables

2.59   The coding of mathematics and tables is so complex and so exacting that, at least at the present time, a text perfectly prepared for one typesetter is likely to be completely unusable by another. Until completion of the AAP Electronic Manuscript Project (see 2.2), which is addressing as separate modules the preparation and coding of mathematics and tables, the option of electronic processing by a commercial typesetter is not really open to the authors of heavily mathematical and tabular material unless those authors know from the outset who the typesetter will be. Even authors who are able to get this information from their publishers should consider the magnitude of the project they are taking on. A meticulously coded mathematical or tabular text can result in stunning cost savings, but the price the author must pay in time and effort is comparable.

2.60 *Equations.* At the present time the coding of displayed and other complicated equations should probably be left to the typesetter (for the coding of simpler, run-in mathematical expressions, see 2.81–2.87). However, you can type the equation on your computer and indicate to the typesetter that it will need special attention by coding its beginning and end:

```
<eq>Kab = (k1, k2, k3)</eq>
```

The text preceding the equation should end with a $</p>$ or a carriage return alone, whichever you are using to tag the ends of paragraphs, and the text following the equation should begin on a new line, with a begin-paragraph code if appropriate.

2.61 Displayed equations and other complex material that will be coded by the typesetter should be made to look on the printout the way you want them to look on the typeset proofs. Since the material will be conventionally handled, the typesetter must know what the complex material, in this case the displayed equation, is to look like in the finished book. Hence, even if you are using the generic codes for superscripts and subscripts elsewhere (see 2.93–2.96), you should use your machine superscript and subscript commands, if you have them, within these displayed equations. If you do not have these machine commands, you will have to resort to inserting the sups and subs by hand or typing the whole formula out at a typewriter and cutting and pasting it onto the printout.

2.62 *Tables.* Because of the difficulty of coding tables properly, most publishers and typesetters are still recommending that you not attempt to add coding to the tables you prepare electronically. Tables should be prepared and stored in a separate file, cross-referenced to the appropriate part of the text (see 1.75–1.77).

2.63 If, after reading 2.59 and 2.62, you are still interested in coding your tables for electronic processing, you should consult with your publisher for appropriate instructions.

Notes

2.64 Whether the notes are to be endnotes or footnotes in the finished book, they should be prepared in a separate file (see 1.78–1.83).

2.65   For *footnotes,* group the notes by chapter and precede each chapter's notes with something like the following:

```
<!Chapter One Notes!>
```

Note that such a message should be handled as a nonprinting comment (see 2.107).

2.66   For *endnotes,* group the notes by chapter and code the headings as follows, changing the chapter number as appropriate:

```
<nth1>Chapter One</>
```

The code <nth1> (with a "one," not an "el") stands for a first-level note subhead. The code </> is the exit code for all display type (see 2.26 and 2.37).

2.67   Authors who do not know yet whether they will be having footnotes or endnotes should follow the instructions for footnotes.

2.68   Within the text of a note, titles of books and journals should be identified with the codes recommended for italics (see 1.44 and 2.38–2.42).

2.69   Within the notes file, the first note in each chapter should be preceded with the code <nttx> (for "notes text") and should end with a </p> or a carriage return alone, whichever you are using as an end-of-paragraph indicator. Each subsequent note within a chapter should begin with a begin-paragraph code and end with a </p> or carriage return alone. The final note in each chapter, as well as the last note in the file, should end with the exit code </>.

```
<!Chapter One Notes!>

<nttx>1. M. Gitelson, "On the Identity Crisis in

American Psychoanalysis," <i>Journal of the American

Psychoanalytic Association</i> 12 (1964): 460.</p>

    <p>2. L. Stone, <i>The Psychoanalytic Situation:

An Examination of Its Development and Essential

Nature</i> (New York: International Universities

Press, 1962), 56.</p>

    <p>3. H. Kohut and E. Wolf, "The Disorders of the
```

```
Self and Their Treatment: An Outline,"

<i>International Journal of Psychoanalysis</i> 59

(1978): 424.</>

<!Chapter Two Notes!>
```

2.70   Discursive notes should be handled the same way as bibliographic notes. The first note in each chapter should begin with
the code <nttx> and should end with a </p>, or a carriage
return alone. Each subsequent note, or each successive paragraph within a note, should start with a begin-paragraph code
and should end with a </p> or carriage return. The final note
in each chapter, and the final note in the file, should end with
the exit code, </>.

2.71   Block quotations within a note should be coded the same way as
block quotations in text (see 2.46–2.50), except that the beginning of the note quotation should be coded with <ntbq> (for
"notes block quotation"). The end of the quotation should be
identified with </>.

Bibliographies

2.72   Bibliographies should be prepared in a separate file (see 1.84).
The first entry in the bibliography should begin with the code
<bibtx> (for "bibliographic text"); each subsequent entry should
start with a begin-paragraph code. Each entry should end with a
</p> or a carriage return alone. The final entry in the bibliog-
raphy should end with the exit code </>.

```
<bibtx>Ballou, E. B. 1970. <i>The building of the

house: Houghton Mifflin's formative years.</i>

Boston: Houghton Mifflin.</p>

    <p>Sheehan, D. 1952. <i>This was publishing: A

chronicle of the book trade in the gilded age.</i>

Bloomington: Indiana University Press.</>
```

See also 2.37.

2.73   Titles of books and journals within the bibliography should be
coded as italic or underlined (see 1.44 and 2.38–2.42).

2.74   If the bibliography is to be grouped into sections (for example, primary and secondary sources), the subheads of the bibliography can be labeled as first-level bibliography subheads or second-level bibliography subheads, using the codes <bibh1> (with a "one") or <bibh2>. Each bibliography subhead should end with the exit code </>. The first entry within a section of the bibliography should be preceded with the code <bibtx> and should end with a </p> or a carriage return alone. Each subsequent entry in a section should start with a begin-paragraph code and end with a </p> or a carriage return alone. The last entry in a section, as well as the last entry in the bibliography, should end with an exit code, </>.

```
<bibh1>Printed Sources</>

<bibtx>Ames, W. L., and K. S. Thorne. 1968. The

optical appearance of a star that is collapsing

through its gravitational radius. <i>Astrophysical

Journal</i> 151:659.</p>

    <p>Hocking, J. G., and G. S. Young. 1961.

<i>Topology.</i> Reading: Addison-Wesley.</p>

    <p>Kobayashi, S., and K. Nomizu. 1963.

<i>Foundations of differential geometry,</i> vol. 1.

New York: Interscience.</p>

    <p>Penrose, R., and W. Rindler. 1984. <i>Spinors

and space-time.</i> Vol. 1, <i>Two-spinor calculus

and relativistic fields.</i> Cambridge: Cambridge

University Press.</>

<bibh1>Interviews</>
```

Figure Legends

2.75   Figure legends should be prepared in a separate file (see 1.86). The first legend should begin with the code <fig> and end with a </p> or a carriage return alone. Each subsequent legend should be typed paragraph style and should end with a </p> or a carriage return alone. The last legend in the file should end with an exit code, </>. There should be no extra space left between legends.

```
<fig>Fig. 1. Pam and Jennie at Bob's birthday
party.</p>
    <p>Fig. 2. Liz at the NBI keyboard, demonstrating
to an attentive audience some applications of the
stored keystrokes feature.</p>
    <p>Fig. 3. Margaret with her five cats and one
dog.</>
```

SPECIAL CHARACTER CODES

2.76   Some characters require coding because they are not commonly available on computer keyboards (e.g., math characters); some require coding when the symbols themselves have been used for other purposes (e.g., when angle brackets are used as code delimiters); some require coding because the internal codes made by the word processor's special treatment keys do not easily translate to typesetting codes.

2.77   Many computers on the market today include what are called "extended character sets" that allow the user to display (and print) a number of special characters in addition to those on the standard keyboard. Unfortunately, many of these extended sets, particularly the Greek letters, are not usable by typesetting computers. Only the typesetting test of a sample disk or tape can determine whether the typesetting computer can hook on to the machine codes that are made everytime a user produces an extended character on his or her system.

2.78   Special character codes are used to designate math characters, Greek letters, or other characters that may not be available on a keyboard or, if they are, may not be usable by the typesetter. The codes take the place of the character or symbol wanted. The codes should be enclosed in delimiters and should be typed wherever the character should appear. No exit codes are necessary.

2.79   Many kinds of special characters can be coded: music symbols, Greek or other foreign language characters, phonetic symbols, scientific notation. Some authors have found coding for special characters to be preferable to the tedious practice of leaving space and then writing the character in by hand. However, you should keep in mind that heavily coded material can be exceedingly difficult to type and almost impossible to proofread. The codes recommended here should be used only in texts with few special characters. Authors who wish to code complicated material should consult with their publishers for specific instructions (see 1.73–1.74).

2.80 Generic codes for a number of frequently used special characters are included in Appendix D of this guide. If your text includes special characters not listed in this appendix, see 2.9 on how to devise your own codes.

Mathematical Expressions and Greek Letters

2.81 You can code individual occurrences of math characters in text and simple, run-in equations as well. However, heavily mathematical text and displayed equations are best left to the typesetter or publishing specialists (see 2.59 and 3.19).

2.82 You should keep in mind that many of the letters in mathematical expressions are conventionally set in italic type. Hence you should use the generic codes for italic or the word processor's underline command for any such letters (see 2.38 and 2.86–2.87).

2.83 If you need to use Greek characters in mathematical expressions, you should spell out the name of the character required. The name of the character should be typed in place of the character wanted and should be enclosed in angle brackets. A lowercase Greek letter should be spelled out in lowercase letters and an upper-case Greek letter in all capitals:

Letter	Code	Letter	Code
α	\<alpha\>		
β	\<beta\>		
γ	\<gamma\>	Γ	\<GAMMA\>
δ	\<delta\>	Δ	\<DELTA\>
ε	\<epsilon\>		
ζ	\<zeta\>		

Letter	Code	Letter	Code
η	\<eta\>		
θ	\<theta\>	Θ	\<THETA\>
ι	\<iota\>		
κ	\<kappa\>		
λ	\<lambda\>	Λ	\<LAMBDA\>
μ	\<mu\>		
ν	\<nu\>		
ξ	\<xi\>	Ξ	\<XI\>
ο	\<omicron\>		
π	\<pi\>	Π	\<PI\>
ρ	\<rho\>		
σ	\<sigma\>	Σ	\<SIGMA\>
τ	\<tau\>		
υ	\<upsilon\>	Υ	\<UPSILON\>
φ	\<phi\>	Φ	\<PHI\>
χ	\<chi\>		
ψ	\<psi\>	Ψ	\<PSI\>
ω	\<omega\>	Ω	\<OMEGA\>

2.84 The following codes for old-style or variant characters are used in math but never in Greek language script:

Letter	Code	Letter	Code
∂	\<osdelta\>	ϱ	\<osrho\>
ε	\<osepsilon\>	ς	\<ossigma\>
ϑ	\<ostheta\>	φ	\<osphi\>
ϖ	\<ospi\>		

2.85   Recommended mathematical codes:

Code	Description	Symbol
<minus>	Minus	−
+	The plus sign, available on standard keyboards (no delimiters necessary)	+
<times>	Multiplication sign	×
/	Division slash, available on standard keyboards (no delimiters necessary)	/
=	The equals sign, available on standard keyboards (no delimiters necessary)	=
<gt>	Greater than	>
<lt>	Less than (with an "el")	<
<gte>	Greater than or equal to	≥
<lte>	Less than or equal to (with an "el")	≤
<ds>	Division sign	÷

2.86   The special character code should be typed in place of the character wanted:

x = exp(a <minus> b)

will be typeset as

$x = \exp(a - b)$

2.87   Unless your publisher instructs you otherwise, you should leave a space before and after the code for each operational sign.

a<omega> <gte> <SIGMA> +
(1/<i>n</i>)

will be typeset as

$a\omega \geq \Sigma + (1/n)$

Greek Words and Phrases in Text

2.88   If you need to identify Greek words or phrases used in text, as opposed to individual Greek letters used in math, you should use the codes <gk> and </gk> to identify the beginning and end of the Greek word or phrase. Then transliterate the Greek passage into the corresponding Latin characters, using the transliteration table that appears as table 1.

```
<gk>bia</gk>
```

will be typeset as

βια

Table 1. Table for coding Greek words and phrases

Name of Letter	Lowercase Greek	Code	Uppercase Greek	Code
Alpha	α	a	A	A
Beta	β	b	B	B
Gamma	γ	g	Γ	G
Delta	δ	d	Δ	D
Epsilon	ε	e	E	E
Zeta	ζ	z	Z	Z
Eta	η	h	H	H
Theta	θ	j	Θ	J
Iota	ι	i	I	I
Kappa	κ	k	K	K
Lambda	λ	l	Λ	L
Mu	μ	m	M	M
Nu	ν	n	N	N
Xi	ξ	x	Ξ	X
Omicron	o	o	O	O
Pi	π	p	Π	P
Rho	ρ	r	P	R
Sigma	σ	s	Σ	S
Terminal sigma	ς	q		
Tau	τ	t	T	T
Upsilon	υ	u	Υ	U
Phi	φ	f	Φ	F
Chi	χ	c	X	C
Psi	ψ	y	Ψ	Y
Omega	ω	w	Ω	W

2.89 Ask your publisher for instructions on how to code the Greek accents and breathing marks.

Diacritical Marks

2.90 Codes for diacritical marks are used to produce accented characters. A diacritic code is typed immediately before the letter it will accent; it indicates to the typesetting computer that the character following the code receives the accent. For example,

tête

is typed

```
t<cir>ete
```

2.91 Some computers can produce diacritical marks on either the screen or the printout. These machine-specific marks, however, may not be usable by the typesetter. Only the typesetter's test of the sample disk will tell. If the typesetter cannot use your machine's diacritics, you will have to code them just as if your machine did not have diacritics.

2.92 Recommended diacritic codes:

Code	Description	Symbol
<ac>	acute	é
<bre>	breve	ĭ
<ced>	cedilla	ç
<cir>	circumflex	ê
<gv>	grave	è
<hac>	haček	ǐ
<mac>	macron	ā
<oc>	overcircle	å
<od>	overdot	ṅ
<swe>	Swedish slash	ø
<tid>	tilde	ñ

Code	Description	Symbol
<uc>	undercircle	ḥ̥
<ud>	underdot	ḍ
<um>	umlaut	ö

Superscripts and Subscripts

2.93 Do not assume that because your computer system can produce them you need not code superscripts or subscripts. If you are using a dedicated word processor or microcomputer with word processing software, the typesetting computer will probably be able to recognize your word processing codes for superscripts and subscripts. To be certain, your publisher will need to test a sample disk. If the typesetting computer can recognize your word processing codes, no additional coding will be necessary. However, the word processing codes from many systems do not translate easily, and some systems (especially mainframe computers) do not have these codes at all. If your machine codes cannot be read by the typesetting computer, if you are working on a system that cannot produce superscripts or subscripts, or if you do not yet have a publisher, use the codes suggested here.

2.94 Recommended superscript and subscript codes:

<sup>   superscript

<sub>   subscript

2.95 The codes for superscript and subscript go in front of the character to be raised or lowered and indicate to the typesetting computer that the character immediately following the code requires special treatment. No exit codes are necessary.

H_2O	should be typed as	H<sub>2O
invasion[3]	should be typed as	invasion<sup>3

2.96 The codes for superscript and subscript are one-time-only codes; that is, they refer only to the character that immediately follows the code. This is why they need no exit codes. For two-digit note references, the code must be typed twice:

footnote reference.[27]

should be typed as

```
footnote reference.<sup>2<sup>7
```

Hyphens and Dashes

2.97   The codes recommended for hyphens and dashes, in order of
increasing length, are

-	Hyphen; no code needed
<n>	En dash, used between inclusive numbers
--	Standard dash; two hyphens with no space before or after
<3m>	3-em dash, the long dash used for successive works by the same author in a reference list or bibliography

2.98   The ordinary hyphen used within compound words needs no
code. It should not be confused with the en dash or the standard
dash. (See 1.63–1.64.)

2.99   The en dash is not available on standard keyboards but is used
in type. It is longer than a hyphen but shorter than a standard
dash, and is used for the most part between inclusive numbers.
There should be no space before or after the code.

```
1969<n>79

pages 66<n>82
```

The copyeditor will mark other instances of the en dash on the
edited printout.

2.100   The standard dash (called an em dash in typesetting terminology)
can be indicated the same way it is in typewritten text, as two
hyphens with no space preceding or following them:

```
The Dudleys had three children--Philippe Serpel,

Winifred Sara, and Julian Tom.
```

2.101   The 3-em dash should be typed immediately after the begin-
paragraph code and should be followed by a period or a comma:

```
<p>McKeon, Richard. "Aristotle's Conception of the

Development and the Nature of Scientific Method."
```

```
<i>Journal of the History of Ideas</i> 8 (1947):

3<n>44.</p>

    <p><3m>. <i>The Philosophy of Spinoza: The Unity

of His Thought.</i> New York: Longmans, Green,

1928.</p>

    <p><3m>, ed. <i>The Basic Works of

Aristotle.</i> New York: Random House, 1941.</p>
```

The above coding would very likely be used to produce the following typeset version:

> McKeon, Richard. "Aristotle's Conception of the Development and the Nature of Scientific Method." *Journal of the History of Ideas* 8 (1947): 3–44.
> ———. *The Philosophy of Spinoza: The Unity of His Thought.* New York: Longmans, Green, 1928.
> ———, ed. *The Basic Works of Aristotle.* New York: Random House, 1941.

En Space

2.102 The code for "en space," <ns>, which is used in front of the single digits in a list of ten or more items, is discussed in 2.57.

Symbols Used as Codes

2.103 When symbols have been used as codes or delimiters, occurrences of those symbols in text must be coded. The codes should be typed wherever the symbol would occur in text. Of course, any symbol that will occur frequently in text should not be used as a code.

2.104 Recommended symbol codes:

<gt>	greater than	>
<lt>	less than (with an "el")	<

2.105 If you have used angle brackets as delimiters, any angle brackets used to represent "greater than" or "less than" in text should be identified by the codes indicated above. The code should be typed in place of the character required. If the text requires many angle brackets, you may wish to use a different set of characters (such as braces) as code delimiters (see 2.13–2.17).

"HELP" CODES

2.106 If your text contains something that is not covered anywhere in this guide, you should ask your publisher for guidance. If you do not yet have a publisher or if your publisher does not know how to code the material in question, you should precede it with a <help> code and end it with </help>. Type the material itself the way you want it to look in print.

```
Accommodations are available at the following
hotels:</p>
        <help>   Ritz-Carlton Hotel    266-1000
                 Whitehall Hotel       944-6300
                 Raphael Hotel         943-5000</help>
```

Within "help" codes there is good reason for ignoring the usual rule against decorative formatting. Here the typesetter will be doing the coding. The "help" code is a plea for skilled human intervention, and the skilled human needs to know how you want the material to look in the finished book.

NONPRINTING COMMENTS

2.107 Comments to the publisher or typesetter that are not meant to appear in the typeset proofs should begin with <! and should end with !> as illustrated in the following:

```
end of text paragraph.</p>
<!Figure 10.1 about here!>
    <p>Text resumes here . . .
```

Comments should begin on a new line and should fall between paragraphs. Do not insert them within paragraphs. To do so could cause problems for the typesetter. That such comments are included in your electronic manuscript should be noted on the list of codes you turn in to your publisher (see 1.139 and 1.110).

FINISHING UP

2.108 When you have finished adding the editing and coding to the electronic version of your manuscript and are proofing the new printout against the edited printout, please check your coding as well. You will want to look out for the following:

1. typographic errors in codes,
2. code delimiters inadvertently used as text symbols,
3. </p> codes missing from the ends of paragraphs and from other line endings that must be maintained in type, if you are using them instead of carriage returns alone, and
4. missing exit codes; there must be an exit code for each entry code (especially important when switching back and forth between roman and italic type!)

2.109 If you have a spelling checker and it is possible to use it to check the codes, add the codes, including the delimiters, to your dictionary before running the spelling checker.

2.110 When you turn in your printout for editing, include a complete list of the codes you have used, even if you have used the codes recommended by your publisher. Do not list codes that were recommended but not used (see 1.139). Later, when you send your publisher your final magnetic tape or disks, send an updated, comprehensive list of the codes you have used. This is the list the typesetter will use to translate your generic codes to specific typesetting codes.

SAMPLES

2.111 Samples A, B, and C present examples of a manuscript that has been conventionally typed, generically coded, and typeset electronically.

CHAPTER 2

STYLE

An epigraph at the head of a chapter may be set in italics in the same size type as the text or in roman a size smaller than the text.

The Chicago Manual of Style, 13th ed.

Punctuation

Punctuation marks should generally be printed in the same style or font of type as the word, letter, character, or symbol immediately preceding them:

Johnson 1976a,

Yes!

Has Jean ever read War and Peace?

Quotations

Quotations may be incorporated in the text in two ways: (1) run in, that is, in the same type size as the text and enclosed in quotation marks . . . ; or (2) set off from the text, without quotation marks.

Whether to run in or set off a quotation is commonly determined by its length. In general, quoted matter that runs to eight or ten typed lines is set off from the text; shorter quotations are run into the text. Material set off from the text as a block quotation is not enclosed in quotation marks. Any

SAMPLE A: *Typed manuscript*

quoted matter within a block quotation should be enclosed in double quotation marks, even if the source quoted uses single marks.[10]

Ellipses

Three dots indicate an omission within a sentence or between the first and last words of a quoted fragment of a sentence. Four dots--a period, followed by three spaced dots--indicate the omission of (1) the last part of a quoted sentence, (2) the first part of the next sentence, (3) a whole sentence or more, or (4) a whole paragraph or more.

Special Characters

Diacritics

Names of diacritical marks most commonly used in European and Asian languages written in the Latin alphabet are acute accent (é), grave accent (è), diaeresis or umlaut (ü), circumflex (ê), tilde (ñ), cedilla (ç), macron (ē), and breve (ĕ).

Brackets

Brackets are used to enclose editorial interpolations, corrections, explanations, or comments in quoted material: "Brackets should be used as parentheses within parentheses."

For additional information, authors should consult The Chicago Manual of Style.

SAMPLE A *(continued)*

```
<cn>Chapter 2</>

<ct>Style</>

<ep>An epigraph at the head of a chapter may be set in
italics in the same size type as the text or in roman a
size smaller than the text.</p>

<eps><i>The Chicago Manual of Style,</i> 13th
ed.</>

<h1>Punctuation</>

    <p>Punctuation marks should generally be printed in
the same style or font of type as the word, letter,
character, or symbol immediately preceding them:</p>

<l>Johnson 1976<i>a,</i></p>

<i>Yes!</i></p>

Has Jean ever read <i>War and Peace?</i></>

<h1>Quotations</>

    <p>Quotations may be incorporated in the text in
two ways: (1) run in, that is, in the same type size
as the text and enclosed in quotation marks . . . ; or
(2) set off from the text, without quotation
marks.</p>

<bq>Whether to run in or set off a quotation is
commonly determined by its length. In general, quoted
matter that runs to eight or ten typed lines is set
off from the text; shorter quotations are run into the
text. Material set off from the text as a block
quotation is not enclosed in quotation marks. Any
quoted matter within a block quotation should be
```

SAMPLE B: *Manuscript with generic coding*

enclosed in double quotation marks, even if the source
quoted uses single marks.<sup>1<sup>0</>

<h2>Ellipses</>

Three dots indicate an omission within a sentence
or between the first and last words of a quoted fragment
of a sentence. Four dots—a period, followed by three
spaced dots—indicate an omission of (1) the last part
of a quoted sentence, (2) the first part of the next
sentence, (3) a whole sentence or more, or (4) a whole
paragraph or more.

<h1>Special Characters</>
<h2>Diacritics</>

Names of diacritical marks most commonly used in
European and Asian languages written in the Latin
alphabet are acute accent (<ac>e), grave accent
(<gv>e), diaeresis or umlaut (<um>u), circumflex
(<cir>e), tilde (<tid>n), cedilla (<ced>c), macron
(<mac>e), and breve (<bre>e).

<h2>Brackets</>

Brackets are used to enclose editorial
interpolations, corrections, explanations, or comments
in quoted material: "Brackets should be used as
parentheses within parentheses."

<sp>

For additional information, authors should consult
The Chicago Manual of Style.

<eof>

SAMPLE B *(continued)*

2
Style

An epigraph at the head of a chapter may be set in italics
in the same size type as the text or in roman a size smaller
than the text.

The Chicago Manual of Style, 13th ed.

Punctuation

Punctuation marks should generally be printed in the same style
or font of type as the word, letter, character, or symbol immediately preceding them:

> Johnson 1976*a,*
> *Yes!*
> Has Jean ever read *War and Peace?*

Quotations

Quotations may be incorporated in the text in two ways: (1)
run in, that is, in the same type size as the text and enclosed in
quotation marks . . . ; or (2) set off from the text, without quotation marks.

Whether to run in or set off a quotation is commonly determined
by its length. In general, quoted matter that runs to eight or ten
typed lines is set off from the text; shorter quotations are run into
the text. Material set off from the text as a block quotation is not
enclosed in quotation marks. Any quoted matter within a block
quotation should be enclosed in double quotation marks, even if the
source quoted uses single marks.[10]

Ellipses

Three dots indicate an omission within a sentence or between
the first and last words of a quoted fragment of a sentence. Four
dots—a period, followed by three spaced dots—indicate an
omission of (1) the last part of a quoted sentence, (2) the first
part of the next sentence, (3) a· whole sentence or more, or (4)
a whole paragraph or more.

SAMPLE C: *Typeset proofs*

Special Characters

Diacritics

Names of diacritical marks most commonly used in European and Asian languages written in the Latin alphabet are acute accent (é), grave accent (è), diaeresis or umlaut (ü), circumflex (ê), tilde (ñ), cedilla (ç), macron (ē), and breve (ĕ).

Brackets

Brackets are used to enclose editorial interpolations, corrections, explanations, or comments in quoted material: "Brackets should be used as parentheses within parentheses."

For additional information, authors should consult *The Chicago Manual of Style*.

SAMPLE C *(continued)*

3 Notes to Publishers

3.1   In chapter 3 of this book we address the publisher and present information about how electronic manuscripts fit into the publishing process. In an overview of the steps involved in electronic bookmaking at the University of Chicago Press, we detail some of the particular responsibilities of the acquisitions editor, the copyeditor, the designer, and the production coordinator. It is essential for any member of the publishing team using this guide to read chapters 1 and 2 before proceeding with chapter 3.

3.2   Only a few years ago, many people in publishing expected the new technology to make dramatic savings in money and time. Enthusiasts claimed that some of the steps of traditional bookmaking would be eliminated and that publishers would do away with keyboarding at the typesetter's and proofreading at all stages. Captured keystrokes would inaugurate an era of shorter schedules and greatly reduced costs.

3.3   Current opinion is less optimistic and more measured. Publishers realize that typesetting costs can be significantly reduced when the typesetter does not have to rekeyboard, but that these savings can be offset by additional time spent in the house by staff who are not familiar with the requirements of electronic manuscripts. This section describes the procedures developed at the Press to help equip the staff and the typesetter with the necessary information to process an electronic manuscript without mishap. Although we cannot guarantee that our procedures are foolproof or that they cover every eventuality, we pass along the experience we have gained in our six years of processing manuscripts electronically. With a realistic appreciation of what electronic processing can offer, publishers will be in a much better position to evaluate their choices and to make the new computer technology work for them.

ELECTRONIC OR CONVENTIONAL PROCESSING?

3.4   Whether to use an author's disks or tape for typesetting should be a joint decision made by the acquisitions, copyediting, and production departments as part of the overall publishing plan. The decision should be made as early as possible in the publication process—certainly before the author has turned in a final draft of the manuscript for copyediting.

3.5   The considerations to keep in mind when making this decision are

1. the author's equipment and software,
2. the level of complexity of the text,
3. the amount of editing the manuscript will require,
4. who will add the editing and coding to the electronic files,
5. the schedule of the book,
6. the available time of knowledgeable staff, and
7. the importance of typesetting costs in the price of the book.

EQUIPMENT COMPATIBILITY

3.6   The first question one must ask about an electronic manuscript is, What kind of equipment was used? The publisher can then determine whether the author's equipment is compatible with the publisher's in-house editing equipment or with the typesetter's composition system. The first step is to find out exactly what system and software the author has used. The University of Chicago Press sends a questionnaire to its authors to obtain this essential information (see Appendix A).

3.7   The publisher should also ask whether the author has prepared the whole manuscript on one system, using one word processing or formatting package. If the manuscript has been prepared on more than one system and large sections must be retyped in order to transfer the complete manuscript to one system, the publisher should consider conventional typesetting.

3.8   If the author's equipment is compatible with the publishing or typesetting system, or can be made compatible through a conversion process or through telecommunications (see 3.42), the publisher must determine next whether the nature of the text and the initial preparation of the manuscript make it a candidate for electronic processing.

3.9   If the author's equipment cannot be made compatible with the publishing or typesetting equipment, other arrangements must be made: either the manuscript can be retyped (or scanned) into the publisher's system, or the manuscript can be typeset conventionally.

Which Is Better, Disks or Tape?

3.10 Because any typesetter that has a computerized phototypesetting system can accept magnetic tape, provided it is prepared in a reasonable way, the Press was often told during its first two years of handling electronic manuscripts that magnetic tape was the preferred medium. Now, however, typesetters and conversion service bureaus have expanded their libraries of conversion software to such an extent that the disks of countless systems are readable and usable. In a study of its manuscripts that had been processed electronically, the Press found that whether manuscripts came in on tape or disks, the final typesetting charges were not affected. Unless the author is working with an unusual configuration of hardware and software, disks and tape are equally acceptable.

NATURE OF TEXT

3.11 Not all kinds of text are well suited to electronic processing. In general, simple text is easier to prepare than complicated text and is thus better suited to successful electronic processing. However, careful electronic preparation of complicated text offers greater benefits to author and publisher than does simple text, by reducing to a greater degree typesetting costs and proofreading.

3.12 Before deciding to process a manuscript electronically, the publisher should examine the manuscript itself (or a representative sample of it) to determine how complicated the text is and what special problems it might present.

Text Categories

3.13 As a guide to text evaluation, we have defined four categories of text and have ranked them in increasing order of complexity and hence difficulty of electronic preparation:

1. straight text
2. illustrated books
3. complicated text
4. mathematical and tabular text

3.14 *Straight text.* The easiest kind of text to prepare and process electronically is straight text. It encompasses most works of fiction and most books in the humanities and social sciences. The text of such a manuscript would be straightforward prose, with perhaps two levels of subheads, short epigraphs or extracts, endnotes, bibliography, and fewer than ten tables or figures.

3.15 *Illustrated books.* Text with illustrations can also be quite suitable for electronic processing. Books in art and the natural sciences fall into this category, which may include some social sciences as well. The text is usually straightforward, but there are many more text elements than occur in a novel or monograph. Although the many graphic elements (photographs, drawings, figures, maps, charts) require sophisticated page makeup on the part of the typesetter and careful attention on the part of the author and publisher, they are not included on the author's disks or tape and therefore do not make the author's text preparation more difficult.

3.16 *Complicated text.* Borderline cases should be evaluated for electronic processing carefully. Examples of complicated text are books in linguistic analysis, foreign language texts, poetry books or plays that require complex formatting, and reference books (dictionaries or encyclopedias) that require many different kinds of typographic treatment. The experienced publisher, editor, or author will be able to prepare complicated text for electronic processing, but doing so requires a great deal of painstaking effort. We advise publishers and authors who have limited experience with electronic manuscripts not to attempt electronic processing of highly complicated text as a first experiment.

3.17 The rewards of transmitting and processing complicated text can be measured more readily than those of preparing more straightforward text. Authors and publishers who wish to invest the necessary time and effort to prepare such material carefully should be encouraged to pursue electronic preparation. Certainly someone who is capable of preparing a complicated manuscript correctly should be able to add editing and coding without introducing new errors.

3.18 *Mathematical and tabular text.* The most difficult text to prepare electronically is mathematical and tabular text (see 2.59). It is by no means impossible, but requires much effort and advance planning. Publishers who specialize in science, economics, or technical social sciences will find that developing procedures for electronic preparation of this material is cost-effective, and authors who prepare this kind of text frequently are likely to find the effort worthwhile. However, book publishers who are confronted only occasionally with the need to set many special characters, displayed equations, and tables will probably find that tabular and mathematical text is better left to the typesetter.

3.19   Some authors doing heavily mathematical text have access to equipment with very sophisticated math formatting and printing capabilities. In such cases publishers might consider using the author's printout as camera-ready copy, a very low cost option compared with either conventional or electronic processing.

COPYEDITING: HOW MUCH WILL BE REQUIRED?

3.20   The copyediting department should determine how much and what sort of editing the manuscript will require. If many passages will be rewritten or there will be many minor changes (if, say, 20 percent or more or the manuscript will have to be changed), the manuscript submitted may not be a good candidate for electronic processing. If, on the other hand, the person slated to add the editing to the electronic medium has no objection to doing extensive retyping and proofreading—say, an assistant or a word processing service hired by an author funded by a grant—electronic processing may be a possibility, even with a manuscript that will be heavily edited.

COPYEDITING: WHO WILL ENTER IT AND HOW?

3.21   The publisher must decide early in the publication process who will be responsible for updating the electronic files after copyediting has been completed. Generally, the editorial changes can be added by the author, the publisher, or the typesetter. Who will do this is a decision that should be made before copyediting begins. If it is to be the author, the division of responsibilities should be spelled out in the contract with the author.

The Author

3.22   If the author has prepared the electronic manuscript carefully from the start, is willing to enter editorial corrections, and has submitted a printout that requires light to moderate editing, he or she may be the most appropriate person to add the editorial changes to the electronic medium.

3.23   On the other side, an author who has been inconsistent during the initial preparation of a manuscript or who will not have the time or resources to add editing changes probably should not be relied upon to prepare the final version.

3.24   An author who has agreed to enter the editing will be in the position of typing in someone else's editorial changes. In a heavily edited manuscript, this may prove to be a difficult situation, unless the author is in complete agreement with the editing and fully understands the responsibilities of electronic processing. In addition to considerations of time and psychology, the publisher should keep in mind one practicality: the greater the number of revisions the author must make, the greater the likelihood that additional errors will be introduced. Thus the publisher should weigh carefully the decision as to whether an author should be asked to prepare the final electronic version of a manuscript that requires heavy editing.

The Publisher

3.25   If the publisher will be responsible for entering the editing, many of the same considerations hold. If the manuscript will require substantial editing, the publisher must decide whether conventional composition is not the better route to take.

The Typesetter

3.26   If neither the author nor the publisher can update the electronic manuscript, the publisher may ask the typesetter to make the editorial changes. The publisher, however, must consider whether the cost of updating the electronic files will exceed the cost of conventional composition. In such cases, conventional composition—having the typesetter rekey the manuscript—may be the appropriate course.

PUBLISHING CHRONOLOGY

THE ACQUISITIONS EDITOR AND THE AUTHOR

3.27   When a manuscript is under serious consideration by a publisher, the acquisitions (or sponsoring) editor should provide the author with advice on the final preparation of the manuscript. The Press gives copies of this guide as early as possible to authors preparing electronic manuscripts. Even if the manuscript is not accepted for publication by the house that gave advice on manuscript preparation, the time an author spends improving the physical preparation of the script is time well spent. A well-prepared manuscript will speed the publication process after acceptance.

3.28 After the manuscript has been accepted for publication, the acquisitions editor should determine what equipment and software the author has used to decide whether the manuscript is a candidate for electronic processing (see Appendix A). If the manuscript will be processed electronically, the editor may need to include in the author's contract terms specifying the division of responsibilities between author and publisher.

3.29 If the author's text is suitable for electronic processing, the acquisitions editor and the author must determine who will add the editing and coding. If the publisher does not have the equipment, the staff, or the time to handle this crucial step and the typesetter's charges would offset the savings of processing the manuscript electronically, then the author may be the only one left to do it. Indeed, in some cases the whole decision to proceed electronically will hinge on the author's willingness—and availability—to add the editing and coding. The acquisitions editor must make it very clear to the author that most of the coding would be added *before* the printout is submitted to the publisher for editing and that the editing—and in some cases additional coding as well—would be added *later*, after copyediting has been completed (see 3.80–3.83).

3.30 Why should an author undertake the extra work of entering editing changes and generic coding? In scholarly publishing the cost of typesetting is one of the major costs of book production, because specialized audiences are small and therefore print runs are also small. The author's help in preparing the electronic manuscript for the typesetter can make a significant difference in the typesetting cost. The Press has often realized savings of 20 percent or more of the typesetting bill when manuscripts have been carefully prepared. This saving is usually seen in the list price of the book, making the work more accessible to the audiences the author hopes to reach. Sometimes the author's help in providing a fully coded electronic manuscript can eliminate the need for raising a subsidy for a very specialized work.

3.31 Will time be saved if the manuscript does not have to be rekeyed at the typesetter's? Many misleading claims have been made about how much time can be saved by processing manuscripts electronically. At the Press, we have found that the total time for editing and production is about the same for an electronic manuscript as for a conventionally typeset book. Significant time can be saved at the typesetter's because the manuscript does not have to be rekeyed, but this time may be offset by the extra time the author may need for initial keyboarding as well as by the additional step of sending the edited printout back to the author to enter editing and final coding. As we gain more experience, we are able to improve on the schedules of electronic manuscripts, but going back to the author for an additional step introduces an element of uncertainty into the schedule.

3.32 What does the author need to know about entering the editing changes and final coding? First, the author will need to know when to expect the edited printout for adding the editing and final coding. The author needs to make time for this step just as much as for checking the edited printout, reading page proofs, and making an index. It is important for the author to find out if he or she will have access to the equipment used for preparing the manuscript at the time that editing and corrections need to be added. This can be a problem when the author is dependent upon institutional equipment or secretarial help, or when he or she has moved. Also, the acquisitions editor should not minimize the amount of time required to update the electronic files, add complete coding, produce a new printout, and proofread the new additions against the edited printout. At the Press three weeks is the usual time allowed for this step, longer if the author is not in the United States. The acquisitions editor must stress that this is not a time for the author to rewrite or make new changes. The edited printout will be the typesetter's master copy, and the author may be charged for alterations if the typesetter finds that the electronic version of the manuscript does not conform to the edited printout. Rather than suffer the double indignity of seeing their latest improvements eliminated and then being charged for the typesetter's work in doing this, authors should take care to see that their copyeditors are informed of new changes that must be added to the manuscript at this point, and should write the changes into the edited printout in a different color from that used by the copyeditor (see 1.114, 3.53, and 3.83).

CONTRACTUAL MATTERS

3.33 The decision to use the author's electronic manuscript for typesetting must include a plan for entering editing and coding (see introduction and 3.21–3.26). If this is to be the author's responsibility, the publisher's contract with the author must be amended to show the division of responsibilities and the publisher's policy about author alterations. Since typesetting costs are generally lower when manuscripts are typeset through electronic transfer, the cost of excessive alterations in proof may be high in relation to the cost of composition. The publisher's standard percentage for author alteration may need to be increased to allow for this difference.

EVALUATING AND TESTING THE ELECTRONIC MEDIA AND MANUSCRIPT

3.34 Whenever an author has prepared a manuscript on computer, the publisher should decide if the manuscript is a candidate for electronic processing. The acquisitions editor will need to arrange for the production and copyediting departments to evaluate the manuscript at an early stage, preferably as soon as the manuscript is accepted for publication. A publisher who expects to handle a number of electronic manuscripts should make sure that there is at least one person in the copyediting department and another in production assigned to give such help to the acquisitions editors and their authors. The time spent in evaluating the manuscript at this early stage is a crucial step in anticipating problems and making a plan for handling the special requirements of each manuscript. It is better to decide at this early stage that a manuscript is not a good candidate for electronic conversion than to struggle with problems that should have been anticipated. If a manuscript is a good candidate for conversion, early planning can help prepare all involved for what is expected of them.

3.35 With complete information about the author's system in hand, the acquisitions editor should consult with the production department about the feasibility of using the author's disks or magnetic tape for typesetting. The production department may be able to determine directly from the information supplied by the editor whether the author's system is compatible with the publisher's or the typesetter's equipment.

3.36 If there is any question of compatibility between the author's system and the typesetter's or publisher's, the acquisitions editor should ask the author to supply a sample disk or tape, with corresponding printout of the electronic manuscript, for testing. The sample manuscript should be representative of the manuscript as a whole and should contain examples of any special features (equations, tables, poetry) the manuscript might have. The disk or tape should contain nothing but the sample for the test; the author should not send his or her working files.

3.37   The production department must send the sample medium and printout to one or more typesetters or conversion bureaus that have agreed to test whether the sample can be read into their system and whether the author's special word processing codes— the carriage return, the three-space paragraph indent, superscripts, accented letters, and any other special characters the author's machinery can produce—can be used instead of generic codes. (A facsimile of the printed form the Press sends along with the samples that are to be tested appears as Appendix B.) The Press usually has the samples tested before any generic codes have been added. The earlier the test is performed, the better.

3.38   The typesetter should be selected as early as possible so that the publisher can seek advice from a specific supplier when the author raises technical questions in the course of preparing the final manuscript.

3.39   *Extended character sets.* Some systems enable the user to type in and display special characters such as diacritics and Greek letters. It cannot be assumed that because a system has this capability these characters can be used by the typesetter. Only the typesetting test of a sample medium can tell (see 2.77).

3.40   *A note on codes specific to word processing programs.* Many word processing programs insert into the text various codes that are specific to these programs. By "specific" we mean that the codes differ not only from brand to brand but also frequently from model to model. These specific codes may or may not appear on the computer screen. Sometimes these specific codes are useful. For example, codes for start and stop underlining and for superscripts may be recognizable by some typesetting computers and may eliminate the need for some generic coding. The usability of the specific codes can be determined when the publisher has the typesetter test a sample magnetic medium. If tests show these specific codes are useful, no final conversions will be necessary before the author sends the magnetic medium to the publisher for typesetting. If the tests are only partly successful, some of the word processor–specific codes may have to be replaced by generic codes. If the test is completely unsuccessful, all these specific codes may have to be converted to generic codes. Note that some word processors make this step easier because they have a function that automatically removes all such codes and converts them to generic-like codes. This procedure creates what is sometimes called an "ASCII format file." (Some people call these files "plain" or "pure" ASCII files.) In such cases a new test after conversion to an ASCII format file should be performed to verify compatibility. If the author cannot make the required conversion, conventional processing may be the only answer. If the typesetting test is successful, the publisher must be sure to remind the author to perform the same conversion to ASCII format as a last step, after adding all the editing and removing the page numbers but before sending the medium to the publisher for typesetting. In other words, the final disks or tape the author turns in must conform to the medium that was tested successfully.

3.41   If the medium cannot be read into either the publisher's or the typesetter's system (or cannot be transferred into the system through telecommunications or an intermediate conversion bureau), no further investigation need be made. At this point, the decision is usually made either to set the manuscript conventionally or to rekey it into the publisher's system.

3.42   If both media reading and telecommunications are options, we recommend the former, at least for book-length manuscripts. With telecommunications there is always the risk of losing data and codes en route (see 1.37, 1.42, and 1.47) as well as the possible costliness of transmitting a long manuscript over the telephone lines. In addition, there would be little gained by telecommunicating a manuscript to a typesetter that could not begin the job before receiving the disks or tape in the mails anyhow. Perhaps telecommunications will become a more attractive option for the transmission of long documents as the technology evolves. If telecommunications is the only way of resolving compatibility problems between the author's system and that of the publisher or typesetter, the decision to proceed electronically should not be made until all the risks of telecommunications are weighed and tests are performed.

3.43   If the author's equipment is compatible with the publisher's or typesetter's equipment, the text of the manuscript should be evaluated by the production department to determine the level of complexity (see 3.11–3.18). If a close examination of the manuscript reveals that it is not an appropriate text for electronic processing (even if the author's equipment is compatible with the other systems), other arrangements must be made.

3.44   If the production department finds the manuscript suitable for electronic processing, the copyediting department should examine the manuscript next to determine how much editing will be needed. If editing will be very heavy, the publisher should decide now not to attempt electronic conversion (see 3.20 and 3.24).

3.45   If the decision is made to process the manuscript electronically, the publisher must be sure to tell the author what machine codes are acceptable in place of generic codes, given the results of the typesetting test. The author should be given this information as soon as it becomes available and as soon as the decision is made to proceed electronically. Being able to use machine codes instead of generic codes could save the author valuable time.

PREPARING FOR COPYEDITING

3.46   If there are easily remedied problems with the manuscript preparation, the copyeditor may recommend that the author make any necessary changes before editing begins. Thus the author can often make changes suggested by the publisher and by the manuscript readers at the same time.

3.47   Once a manuscript is scheduled for electronic processing, the copyeditor should waste no time in finding out what the order of events for the project is going to be. Will the author add the editing? Can the author do this work without being tempted to continue rewriting (see 3.32)? Will the author add more coding if it is needed? Will the author proofread the final version of the manuscript, the one with all the codes and editing in place? If not, will anyone do a final proofreading?

3.48   A copyeditor (preferably the person who will later perform or supervise the copyediting) should look at the draft and, if necessary, request any physical changes in the printout—wider margins, double spacing, darker printout, and the like—that will facilitate copyediting.

3.49   The copyeditor may also make suggestions regarding the publisher's house style (use of arabic or roman numerals, British or American spelling, capitalization, hyphenation, and bibliographic style) that the author may incorporate into the final version of the manuscript that will be submitted for copyediting. Obviously, the more correct the version of the manuscript submitted for editing, the more smoothly will editing and production proceed.

3.50   The copyeditor (or the publisher's specialist in electronic publishing) can at this time determine what kinds of generic codes will be necessary to identify text elements within the manuscript and whether any codes will be necessary for diacritics and other special characters. If the text has a large number of diacritics that must be coded, the coding of these characters can be delayed until after editing has been completed so that these codes will not impede the copyeditor's ability to read the script and spot typographical errors. On the other hand, the copyeditor will need to know where the author intends to add the diacritics, so at this stage the author might be asked to add the accents by hand in colored pencil. If the author's machine can produce diacritics and other special characters on the printout but the typesetter that tested the medium was not able to use those machine characters and hence requested generic coding (see 3.39), the author can nevertheless use the machine special characters as a temporary measure to make a more readable printout, if the author is prepared to change these machine codes later to generic codes.

The "Final" Manuscript

3.51 The publisher should take care to inform the author that the final draft, though it may incorporate the changes suggested by readers during the review process as well as preliminary style changes suggested by the copyeditor, is still subject to complete editing by the publisher's copyediting department.

3.52 The ease with which changes can be made on a computer often invites an author to continue working on the electronic manuscript long after the "final" printout has been submitted to the publisher. One should never take it for granted that the printout submitted for copyediting is the latest version of the text. The copyeditor should advise the author not to tinker with the electronic text any more, since the copyeditor must know of all changes.

3.53 The author who wants to make additional changes after submitting the final draft must keep a record of those changes on paper and must submit those changes to the copyeditor during the editing process. Authors who exhibit a tendency to continue revising during the editing process should be given a deadline for such changes and may be warned that editing will not continue until the author has submitted what he or she can assure the publisher is a finished manuscript. Authors may, of course, make changes on the copyedited printout after they have received it for review from the copyeditor. These changes, however, should be made in a colored pencil different from any color so far used on the manuscript so that the copyeditor will be able to spot them easily.

COPYEDITING

3.54　When changes recommended by the manuscript readers and the publisher's editors have been made, the author should deliver a completed manuscript to the acquisitions editor. Front matter will be added by the publisher before the manuscript is scheduled for editing. This front matter consists of half-title page, series page, title page, copyright page, and dedication. Because much of this material is set in display type, and some, such as CIP data, arrives late in the publication process, the Press does not usually ask the author to incorporate this front matter into the electronic manuscript but has these pages typeset conventionally. The Press asks the author to provide copy for the contents page but because of its complexity usually has this conventionally typeset as well. Some publishers may require that front matter be incorporated into the electronic manuscript and fully coded, especially if they have uses for the electronic version of the manuscript other than for typesetting.

3.55　While conscientious copyeditors can benefit from hands-on experience with computers, they need not have any computer experience in order to recognize the black holes of the new technology and avoid stepping in them. Computer savvy or not, copyeditors do need to become familiar with new procedures and routines introduced by electronic manuscripts. If they do not, problems that could have been avoided may arise.

Using the First Chapter as a Test

3.56　It is sometimes impossible to predict that copyediting of a manuscript will be heavy until editing actually begins. Since manuscripts upon which the editing is expected to be heavy are not as a rule good candidates for electronic publication, it should be a responsibility of the copyeditor to report back to the acquisitions and production departments if, after editing a chapter of a manuscript slated for electronic publication, the editing of that chapter has been unexpectedly heavy. In cases where it is discovered that the editing is likely to be heavy, the decision to proceed electronically should be reconsidered. The editor should not wait until editing is finished to inform publishing colleagues of this unexpected development, since production plans, if they are going to be changed, should be changed as early as possible (see 3.20 and 3.24).

Mechanics of Editorial Marking

3.57　In marking up the printout, copyeditors should remember that (1) instead of keying the script character for character, the author or the author's typist will be making changes to something that already exists and (2) the author or the author's typist will more than likely be unfamiliar with the standard proofreading marks used by the copyeditor.

3.58　Because an electronic version of the manuscript already exists, the printout should be marked more as if it were proof than original manuscript. All changes on the printout, especially the small changes, should be made very conspicuous. Never, under any circumstances, use black pen or pencil to do the editing. Instead, use something like fiery red. Special care should be taken to make small changes visible. For instance, never simply add a hyphen or change a period to a comma or a comma to a period. Always flag these small changes with a caret. In fact, make it a habit to use the caret liberally so that none of the small changes will be overlooked. Signal the change of a comma to a semicolon with a boldly inserted caret. Make deletions with a heavy stroke, and never, ever, use white-out material. It might also be helpful to put a checkmark in the left margin of any line containing a change. If the printout includes line numbers, the numbers of lines with changes can be circled. If there is a possibility that some change will be missed, write a note in the margin: "change comma to semicolon," for instance.

3.59　The author of an electronic manuscript—or his or her assistant—may not be familiar with standard proofreading marks. Do not use these marks without explaining them at their first occurrence. Not everyone is likely to know that a circled number should be spelled out or that a handwritten "equal" sign is a request for a hyphen. The copyeditor should not assume that an amateur will understand that a circle around a comma means to use a period or that a caret over a period means to use a comma. So it is important to explain each mark as it occurs or to refer the author or typist to the standard proofreading marks (see fig. 1). Again, add notes in the margin whenever there is likely to be any confusion or misunderstanding about what is intended.

PROOFREADER'S MARKS
OPERATIONAL AND TYPOGRAPHICAL SIGNS

Mark	Meaning	Mark	Meaning
ℐ	Delete	*ital*	Set in *italic* type
◡	Close up; delete space	*rom*	Set in roman type
ℐ	Delete and close up (use only when deleting letters *within* a word)	*bf*	Set in **boldface** type
stet	Let it stand	*lc*	Set in lowercase (uncapitalized)
#	Insert space	*cap*	Set in CAPITAL letters
eq #	Make space between words equal; make leading between lines equal	*sc*	Set in SMALL CAPITALS
hr #	Insert hair space	*wf*	Wrong font; set in correct type
ls	Letterspace	X	Reset broken letter
¶	Begin new paragraph	V	Insert here *or* make superscript (N^2)
□	Move type one em from left or right	∧	Insert here *or* make subscript (N_1)
⌐	Move right		

PUNCTUATION MARKS

Mark	Meaning
⌐	Move right
⌐	Move left
⌐⌐	Center
⊓	Move up
⊔	Move down
fl	Flush left
fr	Flush right
=	Straighten type; align horizontally
‖	Align vertically
tr	Transpose
sp	Spell out

Mark	Meaning
⌃	Insert comma
⌄	Insert apostrophe (or single quotation mark)
⌄ ⌄	Insert quotation marks
⊙	Insert period
set ?	Insert question mark
;/	Insert semicolon
:/	Insert colon
|=|	Insert hyphen
⌶/M	Insert em dash
⌶/N	Insert en dash
(|)	Insert parentheses

Fig. 1. Standard proofreaders' marks. From *The Chicago Manual of Style*, 13th edition, © 1969, 1982 by The University of Chicago.

Should Electronic Manuscripts Be Edited Differently?

3.60   Many publishers, including the University of Chicago Press, are finding it extremely difficult, at least in real life, to answer the question of whether to edit an electronic manuscript differently from the way they would edit a manuscript to be produced conventionally. If the publisher's decision is to handle the editing differently, that is, to do less editing, then perhaps one is justified in asking whether the technology is not being allowed to control the product—and the publisher—rather than vice versa. Should the choice of technology be allowed to lower the quality of the book? Should the medium be allowed to get in the way of the message?

3.61   Another issue complicating the decision to edit electronic manuscripts differently is how far copyeditors can be expected to turn in their best effort in a world in which there are no house rules, in which even the smallest stylistic points must be decided each time. How far can one go in asking editors to abandon a style they are used to and within which they are comfortable and can do their best job? Their job is bound to become harder if they are asked to go along with alternative styles with each book they edit, even though these alternative styles may be quite reasonable in and of themselves. One of the benefits of having a house style is to eliminate the need to make stylistic decisions constantly. This frees copyeditors to focus their attention on substance. "Let's see, now. Has the author been capitalizing the *p* in 'Democratic party' or not? Is it this author who is using the serial comma or was it my last author?" The copyeditor required to edit one book according to one style and another book according to another style will at the very least have to keep a much more extensive style sheet and may require more time to edit the book, even though less editing is being done.

3.62   If the publisher's position is that the same high standards of copyediting should be in effect for all manuscripts, electronic as well as traditional, things seem nicely resolved in theory. But when you get down to actual cases, it becomes very important who is adding the editing to the electronic medium. Unless the publisher has a computer system that is compatible with the author's, and also has the staff that will be needed, the author is, by default, the one responsible for entering the editing changes. If the typesetter makes the changes, the publisher is apt to lose the cost savings that might be realized by producing the manuscript electronically. It is because the author is taking over much of the former role of the typesetter that savings can be made. However, it will be very awkward indeed to insist that the author make every little change—as well as every large one. After all, it is the author whose prose is being tampered with, whose stylistic decisions are being overruled, and whose training is very rarely in the field of typesetting.

What Are Some of the Things That Can Be Done Differently?

3.63   If the publisher adopts a flexible stance with regard to the copyediting of electronic manuscripts, there are certain mechanical or arbitrary things that a copyeditor does to conform to house style— things that, if done in some other consistent, reasonable way, should not detract from the quality of the writing. Copyeditors will not always agree on what these things are. We have put together the following list of possible stylistic variables for consideration of copyeditors, who are free of course to pick and choose among them according to their degree of agreement with each one:

—Use or nonuse of the serial comma

—What abbreviations to spell out (U.S., U.K., etc., e.g., i.e.)

—The transposition of dates (May 7, 1985, to 7 May 1985, for example)

—Permissibility of British spellings (although the author could convert these spellings globally, this may be a dangerous practice unless there is no quoted material in the manuscript containing British spellings or unless the author can effect the global changes on an instance-by-instance basis; see 1.21–1.25)

—Acceptability of alternative reference and bibliographic styles

—Spelling out of numbers or using numerals

—Capitalization style, particularly regarding the words "chapter," "appendix," "table," "figure," "equation," and "part"

—Spelling out "percent" or using the symbol

—The handling of a source at the end of an extract (e.g., using brackets or parentheses, placing the source inside or outside the quote's final punctuation, placing the poetry source on a line by itself)

—In manuscripts with some foreign text, ways of handling English translations

—Deletion or inclusion of commas after introductory clauses and phrases (thus, therefore, hence)

—Inclusive number style (123–124 or 123–24)

3.64   In addition, the copyeditor could refrain from making some changes that, in a manuscript to be produced conventionally, would be made in the interest of a more felicitous phrasing or a more refined typography. However, the subject matter of such a manuscript should be primarily informational rather than literary. Such changes might include the following:

—The transposition of words not for the sake of meaning but solely for the sake of better syntax or rhythm

—The substitution of en dashes for hyphens between inclusive numbers (for a book with lengthy bibliographical material, such a policy would eliminate for the author considerable additional coding)

—Interchanging ''which'' and ''that''

—Adding space between ellipsis points (however, if the author has mistyped these consistently, the typesetter can use the closed up ellipses as a code to get spaced ellipses, but the ellipses must be included on the list of generic codes turned in by the author that goes eventually to the typesetter)

—Changing ''while'' to ''whereas'' or ''although'' in cases in which the ''while'' is not being used temporally

—Marking letters in mathematical expressions for italics

3.65   At the University of Chicago Press we have no firm policy on whether electronic manuscripts should be edited differently from conventional ones, but for the most part we make this decision on a manuscript-by-manuscript basis. We try to eliminate as prospects for electronic publishing those manuscripts that are likely to cause eventual problems if they are handled electronically: manuscripts likely to need extensive editing and manuscripts whose authors may balk at being asked to enter changes to their prose.

3.66   Whether a manuscript is likely to require extensive editing can sometimes be determined very early in the publishing process, even before the manuscript reaches the copyediting department. With other manuscripts, however, the need for heavy editing escapes detection until copyediting begins, and the copyeditor of a manuscript slated for electronic typesetting should report back to the production and acquisitions departments after editing the first chapter of the book on just how much editing is being done (see 3.56). If the author is likely to be resistant to typing the editing changes, the copyeditor should probably consult with the acquisitions editor, the only staff member at this point likely to know the author, on how much latitude there may be to make changes on the basis of the author's personality.

3.67 Hence it may be inadvisable to enforce the same editing standards on electronic manuscripts as on conventional manuscripts, at least when the author is entering the changes. First, the more corrections that are required, the greater the possibility that new errors will be introduced. If professional typesetters introduce errors in the process of making changes, of course amateur keyboarders are likely to make errors. Second, when editing has been heavy, the author who has agreed to enter the changes is being put in a very awkward position indeed. The author may see it as adding insult to injury.

Tables and Figures

3.68 Many typesetters still find it helpful to have marginal handwritten notations on where approximately to set each figure and table, so copyeditors should continue this practice, even when the author has typed messages about figure and table placement into the electronic manuscript (see 1.76 and 1.87).

3.69 Copyeditors should know whether tables are being handled conventionally, as they usually are at the Press even when the rest of the manuscript is being handled electronically. If they are being handled conventionally, copyeditors should make sure they are included on the list of manuscript elements to be typeset conventionally that is delivered to the typesetter along with the printouts and media. At the Press this information is conveyed to the typesetter via a form (Appendix C), which the author fills out and returns to the publisher for sending to the typesetter.

Em Dashes

3.70 Em dashes, as long as they have been typed as two hyphens with no space preceding or following them, need not be marked in any way. However, the two hyphens should be included on the list of codes prepared by the author that is eventually given to the typesetter. As long as the typesetter knows that two hyphens are being used—consistently and uniquely—to indicate em dashes, no further coding or marking of them is necessary.

End-of-Line Hyphens

3.71 Normally, copyeditors delete and close up temporary end-of-line hyphens (we shall call these ''soft'' hyphens) and underline end-of-line hyphens that are to be retained as part of the spelling of the word (we shall call these ''hard'' hyphens). If it is possible for authors to produce a printout that has no end-of-line hyphens, they should do so (see our instructions to authors in this regard in 1.63–1.64).

3.72 If the printout does have some end-of-line hyphens, the copyeditor must ask whether the author has used a hyphenation program (a program that tells the computer where to split words that are too long to fit on a line) or strictly hard hyphens (some hyphenation programs only split words with hard hyphens).

3.73 If the editing copy contains only hard hyphens, the only marking that is necessary is to indicate any hyphens that should be deleted and then to instruct the author on whether the components are to be closed up into one word or left as two words.

3.74 If the printout contains both soft and hard hyphens, the first thing to do is determine whether the author can furnish a revised printout without end-of-line hyphens. If this is impossible, the copyeditor is faced with a situation in which the printout makes no distinction between hard and soft hyphens, and only the computer knows which is which. One way of proceeding would be to mark the end-of-line hyphens as they would be marked conventionally. The person adding editing to the electronic medium would then have to be advised of the meaning of these end-of-line marks and told to make a separate pass through each electronic file dealing strictly with end-of-line hyphens, since only from examining the computer file will the keyboarder be able to tell whether an end-of-line hyphen on the printout is hard or soft.

Unusual Concerns during Copyediting

3.75 *Els versus ones.* Check that the author has not used the letter ''el'' in place of the number ''one'' and vice versa. We stress this rule throughout these pages and ask the copyeditor to get involved in determining whether the author has heeded it because it is one of the most frequently broken rules of electronic manuscript preparation and is disproportionately expensive for the typesetter to repair. There is no simple global way for the typesetter to convert the letter "el" to the number "one" where the number and not the letter is wanted. What makes it so difficult not to break this rule is that many people learned to type on typewriters that had no separate key for the number "one." Hence they learned to use the "el" key for both the letter and the number. Nowadays, when many typewriter as well as computer keyboards do have a separate key for the number, many experienced typists still find it difficult to break the old habit of using the "el" key for both the letter and the number.

3.76 Unfortunately, it may not be easy for the copyeditor to determine whether the rule has been broken or not. This is because the printer used by the author may not distinguish the two characters even though they have been correctly used. If the author's printer does not distinguish els from ones, the copyeditor must throw the ball back to the author and advise the author that it is his or her responsibility to make sure the els and ones have been properly input. (For more on the el versus one problem, see 1.26–1.27.)

3.77 *Checking the generic codes.* Copyeditors should familiarize themselves with the rules of generic coding and electronic manuscript preparation set down in chapters 1 and 2 of this guide. They should make it part of their routine to check that all the codes needed are in place and that no typographic errors have crept into the codes. They should keep a special lookout for missing end codes, such as end-italic codes, end-of-paragraph codes, and the </> exit code that ends display material. Copyeditors should also check that no codes appear in the electronic manuscript that are not included on the list of codes compiled by the author (see 1.139 and 3.84). Codes missing from the list should be added to it and defined for the typesetter. Any codes in the electronic manuscript that are missing from the list of codes will not be programmed by the typesetter for conversion to the desired type style or format. Codes are useless unless they appear on this list. The copyeditor who can examine the manuscript on-line may be able to make the task of code checking less time-consuming.

3.78 The copyeditor should check that no whole subheads are coded for italics. If italics are chosen by the designer as the type style for a particular subhead level, the italics will be taken care of by the structural identifier (<h1>, <h2>, and so on). If there are italic words or phrases within a subhead, see 3.90.

On-Line Editing

3.79 Should the publisher do the editing on-line? This is a subject of much controversy these days. In evaluating such a course, publishers should not overlook the question of authorial review. How is the author going to know how his or her prose has been changed when the editing is done on the screen and a new, completely clean printout is generated? Unless the computer being used has some facility that will flag places in the text where changes have been made, on-line editing may be ill advised for the kind of publishing that relies heavily on the give-and-take between author and copyeditor.

RETURNING THE COPYEDITED MANUSCRIPT TO THE AUTHOR

3.80 After completing the editing, the copyeditor should return the edited printout to the author for approval of editing, answering of queries, and the inclusion of any additional revisions.

3.81 The usual procedure at the Press at this point is for the author, before entering the editing on the disk or tape, to return the edited printout to the copyeditor for final cleanup—copyediting the author's new changes and resolving the points that were queried on the edited printout and have now been answered by the author. This step is equivalent to the final cleanup the copyeditor does in conventional processing just before the manuscript goes to the typesetter for rekeying. In the case of very lightly edited and lightly revised electronic projects and with authors the copyeditor knows are very meticulous, this step may be suspended, however, and any remaining matters that need discussion—such as the appropriateness of the author's last-minute insertions and changes and the resolution of remaining disagreements between the copyeditor and the author—may be taken care of by telephone. This shortcut is risky, though, if there are many author insertions and the insertions themselves may need copyediting.

3.82 At this time the copyeditor should issue some warnings to the author about making global changes that have not been thought out carefully. Global changes to spelling, punctuation, or capitalization should be made only if the author's computer or word processor can make such changes on an instance-by-instance basis and if the device shows the context in which the affected word or phrase occurs. Only in this admittedly slower way can the author change, for example, the capitalization of a particular word so as not to change the word if it also appears in quoted material, at the beginning of a sentence, or within an article or book title (see 1.21–1.25).

ADDING THE EDITING TO THE ELECTRONIC MEDIUM

3.83 After the edited printout has been approved by the publisher, it is returned to the author. It is at this time that the author adds all the editing to the electronic medium and makes the electronic medium agree exactly with the edited printout. The author should be told that, if the project is to stay on schedule, this work must be done as quickly as it can be without introducing new errors, since this is an additional step that is not necessary in conventional processing. The Press generally allows three or more weeks for authors to update their electronic manuscripts. The copyeditor should sternly warn the author at this point not to do further revising other than to correct typographic and factual errors that have so far escaped detection. The author should be told that any corrections of this sort other than simple typos should be discussed by telephone with the copyeditor before they are made and that it is the author's responsibility to write in these corrections on the edited printout, since the typesetter is usually instructed to regard that printout as the master copy (see 3.85). This means that the typesetter will resolve discrepancies between the printout and the electronic version in favor of the edited printout.

3.84 After the author has finished adding the editing to the electronic manuscript, the author should be told to do the following things, in sequence:

1. Back up all files on disks or tape.
2. Run off a clean printout (and, if possible, proofread it against the edited printout).
3. Remove the page numbers from the electronic manuscript.
4. Run a conversion to plain ASCII *if and only if* the sample disk or tape that was tested earlier in the publication process required this conversion (see 3.40).

The author should then send the new printout back to the publisher, along with the edited printout, the electronic medium (disks or tape), the list of file names (see 1.138), an updated list of the codes used (see 1.139), and the information that is requested in Appendix C of this guide.

THE CLEAN PRINTOUT

3.85 Why is the old, edited printout and not the new, clean printout to be regarded by the typesetter as the master copy? The clean printout presumably is an exact record of the electronic version of the manuscript, and any changes on the old printout that were missed by the author when he or she was updating the electronic manuscript, or errors that were introduced in making corrections, will be mirrored in the new printout. Only by checking the old, edited printout against either the electronic version, the new printout, or the typeset proofs can such errors be discovered.

3.86 Since the typesetter is generally instructed to regard the old, edited printout as the master copy and since it is preferable to add the design specifications to the old printout, why is it necessary to have a new printout at all? First and foremost, the new printout serves as a printed record of the updated electronic manuscript that ideally will be proofread against the old printout by the author or at least spot-checked by the copyeditor or someone else appointed by the publisher to spot-check or proofread it. In addition, if there are last-minute errors discovered by the author too late to be added to the medium or errors discovered by the publisher, the corrections can be handwritten on the clean printout and the typesetter instructed to make them. Such corrections would be lost amidst all the other handwriting if they were added to the edited printout. (Publishers should determine in advance how the typesetter is going to bill them for corrections marked on the clean printout.) Having a clean printout that reflects the author's magnetic medium after its final updating can also be useful to the publisher in trying to track down the origin of errors later on. Even typesetters find the clean printout useful for a variety of reasons.

MARKING THE PRINTOUT WITH DESIGN SPECS

3.87 It is at this point that the design specifications should be added to the printout. Unless the edited printout is so heavily marked up that there is no room for the design specifications, the design markup should also be done on this printout. Only when the edited printout is too cluttered with handwriting to permit the addition of the design instructions should the new printout furnished by the author be used for design purposes.

3.88 It is best to keep things as simple as possible for the typesetter, and if you keep all the handwriting, including the design, on the edited printout, the typesetter can regard this copy as the master copy and will not have to keep referring back and forth between two different copies.

3.89 The printout must contain design specifications just as if it were a manuscript destined for conventional typesetting. Remember that the codes are generic, not specific, and they tell the typesetter nothing about the actual design that has been chosen for the book. Hence each element should be identified (''A head'') and given design specifications at its first occurrence, very much in the usual way.

3.90 The copyeditor should check the printout to determine if there is italic coding within subheads, that is, single words or phrases that are underlined or enclosed in generic codes for italics ($<i>$ and $</i>$). If there are, a note informing the typesetter of this should be added to the list of codes provided by the author. Otherwise the wrong font may be used. For instance, if the design calls for first-level subheads to be set in boldface, the italic words within such subheads should probably be in bold italic rather than simply italic. With previous knowledge that an author has done this, the typesetter can conditionally program a conversion of italics within that subhead level to whatever font is appropriate.

PROOFREADING THE UPDATED ELECTRONIC MANUSCRIPT

3.91 One of the most troublesome questions in handling electronic manuscripts is who, if anyone, should do a final proofreading, after the author has added the editing and codes to the electronic medium. On the one hand, it may be cost-ineffective for the publisher to do this; it is an additional, time-consuming step, and publishers' tight schedules often do not permit this extra step. On the other hand, to ask the author to do it may be an imposition; it may also be risky, since it is so easy to overlook errors in one's own copy. A third course, to assume that the updated electronic manuscript is correct and to do no final proofreading, is taking a chance. The Press's course, spot-checking the new printout to determine if there should be a thorough proofreading, has worked well so far, though such a course might not always be a sufficient safeguard.

3.92 Unless the author has proofread his or her changes to the electronic medium—and ideally even when the author has proofread the changes—the copyeditor should use the new, clean printout at least to spot-check that the editing has been added correctly. If the spot-check fails to uncover omissions or new errors made in the process of adding the editing, the manuscript may be considered ready to go to the typesetter. If the spot-check reveals omissions and new errors, then the decision must be made whether extra time should be taken to check the new, clean printout against the edited printout.

DESIGN

3.93 The generic codes recommended in this guide (and the generic codes recommended by other industry groups) are independent of the design; that is, they can be used with any typographic elements or type styles that a designer may choose. The codes do not themselves specify typographic information; the typesetter uses the generic codes in the manuscript for translation to typesetting commands.

3.94 The copyeditor and designer should confer early in the publication process, to examine the manuscript and list any and all text elements that occur in the manuscript. This list of elements can be used by the designer for developing layouts and typographic specifications.

PRODUCTION

3.95 Putting an electronic manuscript into production should not differ considerably from the procedure for conventional manuscripts.

3.96 All relevant pieces of the manuscript should be assembled: the edited printout, the new printout, the floppy disks or magnetic tape, any photographs or other artwork, a list of codes used in the electronic manuscript and their referents, and a list of the file names.

Selecting a Typesetter

3.97 If a sample disk was tested in the early stages of the manuscript evaluation (see 3.36–3.37), the production department should have very clear information about typesetters who can read the disk or tape. Selecting a typesetter that is technically able to work well with a particular electronic manuscript is absolutely crucial. If a disk or tape was not tested earlier, it should now be tested.

3.98   Most typesetters who work with electronic media make lists of the kinds of media they accept. Publishers are urged to ask their typesetting vendors for such information.

Sending the Manuscript to a Typesetter

3.99   The production controller should make every effort to provide the typesetter with as much information as possible about the manuscript and media supplied, such as:

—What medium is being supplied, disk or tape?

—What system was it prepared on?

—Who prepared it, publisher or author?

—Has all the editing been added?

—How much coding has been added?

—Will the typesetter need to add any editorial changes?

—If so, how and where are the changes indicated?

—What sections of the manuscript will be set conventionally (see 1.75 and 3.54)?

3.100   The publisher should be very specific about whether the typesetter is expected to do proofreading of typeset proofs. The policy of many typesetters is not to proofread the output of electronic manuscripts; any such proofreading will be performed at an additional charge. The production controller should take care to come to an agreement with the typesetter about procedures at a very early point, certainly before the typesetter has begun to process the job.

PROOFREADING THE TYPESET PROOFS

3.101   Although authors should be told that it might be possible for them to do a little less proofreading, proofreading should not be suspended altogether. With an electronic project authors should be especially alert for gross errors (passages of computer "garbage" interspersed with the text, for instance), spacing problems, type size problems, paragraph indention errors, problems in the subheads, italic passages that do not end where they should, and, in the worst case, missing text (caused by someone's failure during data transfer to specify a "record length" long enough to accommodate the line lengths used by the author). Some of these errors seem inexplicable, but most of them are the result of human error of one kind or another. Our experience with page proofs in electronic projects has generally been very good, and there have even been a handful of virtually error-free cases. We have heard enough horror stories, however, to know that proofreading should never be dispensed with entirely.

ATTRIBUTING ERRORS IN PROOF

3.102 After galleys or page proofs have been generated, procedures for handling electronic manuscripts are the same as those for handling conventional manuscripts, with the exception of the attribution of errors in proof.

3.103 With electronic manuscripts, since the typesetter presumably did no keyboarding, there are no printers' errors in proofs, at least in the traditional sense. Typos, including generic coding errors, are the responsibility of either the author or the publisher, depending on the terms of the contract. Printers' errors would largely be limited to gross formatting errors or mistakes in following the design. When inexplicable errors creep in, as they occasionally do, a consultation with the typesetter is in order.

3.104 Do not expect author or publisher alterations in proofs to cost less with electronic projects than they do with conventional projects. Once the author's electronic manuscript has been transferred into the typesetter's system and the proofs have been generated, procedures are much the same whether the author's keystrokes were "captured" electronically or the typesetter rekeyed from paper copy. Publishers should expect the same (high) rates they are used to with conventional processing. Billing policy as well as the procedures used for making corrections vary from typesetter to typesetter.

THE ELECTRONIC MANUSCRIPT AFTER TYPESETTING

3.105 Once typesetting is complete, the publisher must decide whether to preserve one or more versions of the electronic manuscript. There are now two electronic versions of the manuscript: the compositor's copy with the typesetter's machine-specific coding and the author's final copy with the generic coding.

3.106 It is important to realize that the author's electronic medium is used by the typesetter only at the outset of processing. The typesetter's first step is to transfer the electronic manuscript from the author's disks or tape into the typesetting computer. From that time on the typesetter works with the version of the text in the typesetting computer, not with the author's disks or tape. Within this (the typesetter's) version, generic codes are converted to specific typesetting codes and (some) corrections are made (but see 3.110). Generally the typesetter makes no changes at all to the author's disks or tape. The original medium remains intact.

3.107 After processing has been completed and the typesetter has returned to the publisher the author's disks or tape, the publisher should return the disks or tape to the author unless some further publishing use for this version is anticipated.

3.108 The publisher that expects to issue revisions or abridgments of the work in the future or has in mind some other use of the electronic medium, such as production of a data base for on-line access or licensing to a software company, must decide whether the typesetter's version or the author's version is more suitable for this purpose.

Using the Typesetter's Copy for Future Editions

3.109 Authors can be involved in creating new editions or abridgments to a greater or lesser extent. If the author of a given project will not be greatly involved in the revision or has little interest in working electronically, the publisher will probably decide to use the typesetter's copy of the electronic manuscript. The production department in this case must make arrangements with the typesetter to preserve this version. Otherwise the typesetter may well erase the book from the typesetting tape and use it for another project.

3.110 If the typesetter's electronic medium is being held for future revisions, the publisher will need to ascertain that the tape incorporates all changes made in page proof because changes are sometimes set conventionally and stripped into the negatives. Since it will be difficult to reconstruct later which changes were made this way, the publisher should be sure to insist that all changes are made in the electronic medium. The publisher will also need to ensure that all corrections made later for reprintings are recorded so that they can be entered into the typesetter's electronic copy of the book at one time when the revision is prepared. Normally it is cheaper to make minor corrections for reprintings by stripping type into negatives; the electronic copy is not used for minor corrections, as such a step would involve costly new page makeup and would compromise the accuracy of the index.

Using the Author's Copy for Future Editions

3.111   If the author's involvement in the revision will be extensive and the author wishes to work electronically, the publisher should ask the typesetter whether the typesetter can reverse the original procedure, that is, whether the typesetter can copy the electronic manuscript on the typesetting tape back to the author's disks or tape. Some typesetters currently are doing this, but transferring back to the original medium anything but a "text stream," a version from which all the codes have been removed, can be a more or less time-consuming process. Because this text stream version lacks all codes—generic and machine formatting codes as well as typesetting codes—the author working with it will have to go through the whole text and reinsert all generic codes and missing machine codes, such as the carriage return. Since we have not yet explored this aspect of the technology, we cannot tell you whether there would be anything gained by this reverse conversion if the result of it is a text stream version. Perhaps it would be easier to devise some method of keeping track of all corrections made after typesetting began and then have the author make these changes to the original disks or tape that went to typesetting. Certainly, scrolling through a book-length text inserting carriage returns would be an extremely tedious process. Publishers interested in doing revisions would be well advised to consult their typesetters as early as possible on what their "downloading" capabilities are. Sometimes a comprehensive reverse conversion can be done and sometimes it cannot.

Appendix A

🏛 University of Chicago Press
Initial Questionnaire for Authors of
Electronic Manuscripts

Author's name _____ Office phone _____

Address _____ Dept. phone _____

_____ Home phone _____

Manuscript title _____

Estimated length of manuscript in typewritten pages _____ or number of words _____

Estimated number of tables _____ illustrations _____

equations: in text _____ displayed _____

mathematical characters: in text _____ displayed _____

diacritics or other special characters _____

Who will type the manuscript if not you? _____

typist's phone(s) _____

Equipment used (check one):

☐ mainframe computer ☐ microcomputer
☐ minicomputer ☐ other _____
☐ word processor

Manufacturer of main hardware _____

Model name and number _____

Operating system _____

Manufacturer of disk drive (if different from above) _____

Manufacturer of printer (if different from above) _____

Type of printer (check one): ☐ dot matrix ☐ daisy wheel ☐ laser ☐ other (explain) _____

_____

Word processing software used and version _____

Text editor _____ Text formatter _____

(continued on reverse)

117

Floppy disks:

Diameter (check one): ☐ 8 inch   ☐ 5¼ inch   ☐ 3½ inch

☐ Single-sided   ☐ Double-sided
☐ Single density   ☐ Double density
☐ Hard-sectored   ☐ Soft-sectored

Estimated number of disks required for your manuscript _____

Magnetic tape:

Can you provide us with a 9-track, 1600 bpi, ASCII tape?   ☐ yes   ☐ no

Can your machine telecommunicate?   ☐ yes   ☐ no

How long will you have access to this equipment? _____

Will you have access to technical (programming) support?   ☐ yes   ☐ no

     programmer's name _____ phone _____

U of C Press house editor's name _____

Date you are returning this questionnaire _____

Date (month and year) you expect to submit completed manuscript to the Press _____

Please return completed questionnaire to your house editor at

     The University of Chicago Press
     5801 South Ellis Avenue
     Chicago, Illinois 60637

To be completed by Press house editor

We have a   ☐ contract   ☐ letter of intent   ☐ other _____

This manuscript will appear on the _____ seasonal list.

Appendix B

🎓 University of Chicago Press
**Electronic Media Evaluation Form
for Typesetters**

To _____ Date _____

_____

_____

From _____

Enclosed is a sample disk/tape and corresponding printout that have been prepared by a
University of Chicago Press author. Would you please test the sample to determine (1)
whether your equipment can read it, and (2) whether any machine codes can be translated to
typesetting codes? Please return the completed form and the sample manuscript to me by
_____.

Author _____

Title _____

Projected date of composition _____ Equipment used _____

Operating system _____ Word processing software _____

Text editor _____ Text formatter _____

Floppy disks

- ☐ 8 inch
- ☐ 5¼ inch
- ☐ 3½ inch

- ☐ single-sided
- ☐ double-sided

- ☐ single density
- ☐ double density

- ☐ hard-sectored
- ☐ soft-sectored

Magnetic tape

- ☐ 9-track
- ☐ 1600 bpi
- ☐ ASCII ☐ EBCDIC

record length _____
number of records _____

block size _____
number of blocks _____

Additional information:

(continued on reverse)

119

To be completed by typesetter

Can you read the sample supplied? ☐ yes   ☐ no

Can you use the machine codes for

ends of paragraphs/carriage returns	☐ yes	☐ no	diacritics	☐ yes	☐ no
italics/underlining	☐ yes	☐ no	other special characters	☐ yes	☐ no
superscripts/footnote references	☐ yes	☐ no	paragraph indent	☐ yes	☐ no
extracts/block quotations	☐ yes	☐ no			

Please comment on any problems you see in the sample:

Signed _____ Date _____

Appendix C

AUTHOR CHECKLIST FOR ELECTRONIC MANUSCRIPTS

🛡 University of Chicago Press
Author Checklist for Electronic Manuscripts

Please complete and return this form with the final electronic version of
your manuscript to your manuscript editor at

> The University of Chicago Press
> 5801 South Ellis Avenue
> Chicago, Illinois 60637

Author _____ Date _____

Title _____

Equipment used _____

Word processing software _____

Author has added ☐ editing   ☐ coding

Enclosed are:

☐ edited printout   ☐ list of file names and contents
☐ new printout   ☐ list of codes used
☐ magnetic medium: ☐ disks   ☐ tape   ☐ all illustrations, photos, maps

Floppy disks: number of disks _____

☐ single-sided   ☐ single density
☐ double-sided   ☐ double density

Magnetic tape:

☐ 9-track   fields: ☐ fixed   ☐ variable
☐ 1600 bits per inch   maximum field length _____
☐ standard ASCII   record length _____
☐ other (specify) _____   number of records _____
    parity: ☐ odd   ☐ even   block size _____
                                       number of blocks _____

List any parts of your manuscript that will be set conventionally and are not on the magnetic
medium (i.e., front matter through table of contents, tables, statistical appendixes, etc.):

Indicate any known problems or inconsistencies with either the text
or the magnetic medium:

Appendix D

Code	End Code	Description
\<ac\>	None[1]	Acute accent[2]
\<acd\>	\</\>	Acknowledgments display title[3]
\<actx\>	\</\>	Acknowledgments text
\<alpha\>	None	Greek alpha, lowercase
\<apd\>	\</\>	Appendix display title[4]
\<apt\>	\</\>	Appendix title, specific[5]
\<aptx\>	\</\>	Appendix text
\<beta\>	None	Greek beta, lowercase
\<bibd\>	\</\>	Bibliography or references display title[6]
\<bibh1\>	\</\>	First-level subhead within bibliography, with a "one"
\<bibh2\>	\</\>	Second-level subhead within bibliography
\<bibtx\>	\</\>	Bibliography or references text[7]

Note: Many of the codes listed here are discussed more fully in the text. For lists of codes by function, see 2.24, 2.83–2.85, 2.92, 2.94, 2.97, and 2.104. The exit code \</\> is used to end all material that differs from the main text, as indicated in this appendix (see 2.26).

1. Codes requiring no exit code either take the place of the character or symbol that is wanted or, as in the case of diacritics, affect only the character immediately following the code.

2. Diacritic codes precede the character to be accented, e.g., l'\<ac\>ecole.

3. The word "Acknowledgments," to be printed at the top of that section of text.

4. The word "Appendix," "Appendix A," "Appendix 1," or the like, to be printed at the top of that section of text.

5. The specific title of this appendix, for example, is Comprehensive List of Codes.

6. The word "Bibliography" (or "References"), to be printed at the top of that section of text.

7. This code directly precedes the first entry in the bibliography (or references) when the bibliography consists of one continuous, alphabetical list without sections. In a bibliography that is divided into sections, the code \<bibtx\> precedes the first entry of each section. The exit code \</\> follows the final bibliographic entry or the last entry of each section.

Code	End Code	Description
<bq>	</>	Block quotation, extract (prose)
<bre>	None	Breve (see note 2)
<ca>	</>	Chapter author (for multiauthor works only)
<ced>	None	Cedilla (see note 2)
<cent>	None	Cent sign ¢
<chi>	None	Greek chi, lowercase
<cir>	None	Circumflex accent (see note 2)
<cn>	</>	Chapter number (e.g., <cn>Chapter 1</>)
<copy>	None	Copyright symbol ©
<cs>	</>	Chapter subtitle
<ct>	</>	Chapter title
<deg>	None	Degree °
<delta>	None	Greek delta, lowercase
<DELTA>	None	Greek delta, cap
<dd>	None	Double dagger ‡[8]
<dpr>	None	Double prime[9]
<ds>	None	Division sign ÷
<dtx>	</>	Dedication page text
<eob>	None	End-of-book generic code
<eof>	None	End-of-file generic code

8. For the superscript, reduced-type version of this symbol, precede this code with the code for superscript.
9. Or arcsecond or second symbol. Do *not* use double quotes. The two are different characters in print.

Code	End Code	Description
<ep>	</>[10]	Epigraph
<eps>	</>	Epigraph source (see note 10)
<epsilon>	None	Greek epsilon, lowercase
<eq>	</eq>	Equation
<eta>	None	Greek eta, lowercase
<e1>	</e1>	First type of emphasized text besides italics, with a "one"
<e2>	</e2>	Second type of emphasized text besides italics
<fig>	</>	Figure legends (see 2.75)
<fwd>	</>	Foreword display title[11]
<fwtx>	</>	Foreword text
<gamma>	None	Greek gamma, lowercase
<GAMMA>	None	Greek gamma, cap
<gds>	None	German double "ess" ß
<gk>	</gk>	Codes to delimit Greek words and phrases (see 2.88)
<gt>	None	Greater than > (see note 14)
<gte>	None	Greater than or equal to ≥
<gv>	None	Grave accent (see note 2)
<hac>	None	Haček (see note 2)

10. If the epigraph is followed by a source, however, the body of the epigraph should end with a </p> or a carriage return alone, whichever is being used to tag the ends of paragraphs, and the source, preceded by the code <eps>, should end with the </> exit code.
11. The word "Foreword," to be printed at the top of that section of text.

Code	End Code	Description
\<help>	\</help>	"Help" code (see 2.106)
\<h1>	\</>	First-level subhead, with a "one"
\<h2>	\</>	Second-level subhead
\<h3>	\</>	Third-level subhead
\<i>	\</i>	Italics[12]
\<iep>	None	Inverted exclamation point ¡
\<ind>	\</>	Introduction display title[13]
\<int>	\</>	Introduction title, specific
\<intx>	\</>	Introduction text
\<iota>	None	Greek iota, lowercase
\<iqm>	None	Inverted question mark ¿
\<kappa>	None	Greek kappa, lowercase
\<l>	\</>	List, unnumbered, with an "el" (see 2.55)
\<lambda>	None	Greek lambda, lowercase
\<LAMBDA>	None	Greek lambda, cap
\<lt>	None	Less than,[14] with an "el," <
\<lte>	None	Less than or equal to, with an "el," ≤
\<mac>	None	Macron (see note 2)

12. Note that punctuation following italicized text should *precede* the end-italics code except in the cases mentioned in the text. See text for discussion of the options for coding italics.

13. The word "Introduction," to be printed at the top of that section of text. These codes are to be used only if the introduction does not carry a chapter number. If the introduction is a numbered chapter, use the chapter codes.

14. To be coded when you want a "less than" symbol to print in your text and you are using < and > as delimiters.

Code	End Code	Description
\<minus\>	None	Minus sign −
\<mu\>	None	Greek mu, lowercase
\<n\>	None	En dash (use this instead of the hyphen between inclusive numbers: 1985\<n\>86)
\<nl\>	\</\>	Numbered list, with an "el" (see 2.56, 2.57)
\<ns\>	None	En space
\<ntbq\>	\</\>	Block quotation, or extract, within a footnote or endnote
\<ntd\>	\</\>	Notes section display[15]
\<nth1\>	\</\>	First-level subhead in endnotes section
\<nttx\>	\</\>	Notes text[16]
\<nu\>	None	Greek nu, lowercase
\<oc\>	None	Overcircle (see note 2)
\<od\>	None	Overdot (see note 2)
\<omega\>	None	Greek omega, lowercase
\<OMEGA\>	None	Greek omega, cap
\<omicron\>	None	Greek omicron, lowercase
\<osdelta\>	None	Old-style Greek delta
\<osepsilon\>	None	Old-style Greek epsilon
\<osphi\>	None	Old-style Greek phi
\<ospi\>	None	Old-style Greek pi
\<osrho\>	None	Old-style Greek rho
\<ossigma\>	None	Old-style Greek sigma
\<ostheta\>	None	Old-style Greek theta

15. The word "Notes," to be printed at the top of the endnotes section.
16. The \<nttx\> code immediately precedes the first footnote, and the \</\> exit code immediately follows the last footnote and precedes the \<eof\> code.

127

Code	End Code	Description
\<p\>	\</p\>	Paragraph[17]
\<pfd\>	\</\>	Preface display title[18]
\<pftx\>	\</\>	Preface text
\<phi\>	None	Greek phi, lowercase
\<PHI\>	None	Greek phi, cap
\<pi\>	None	Greek pi, lowercase
\<PI\>	None	Greek pi, cap
\<pm\>	None	Plus or minus ±
\<pn\>	\</\>	Part number (e.g., \<pn\>Part 1\</\>)
\<po\>	\</\>	Poetry extract (see 2.51–2.54)
\<pound\>	None	Pound sterling
\<pr\>	None	Prime sign[19]
\<psi\>	None	Greek psi, lowercase
\<PSI\>	None	Greek psi, cap
\<pt\>	\</\>	Part title, specific
\<px\>	\</\>	Part text
\<rho\>	None	Greek rho, lowercase
\<sd\>	None	Single dagger † (see note 8)
\<sec\>	None	Section symbol § (see note 8)
\<sigma\>	None	Greek sigma, lowercase
\<SIGMA\>	None	Greek sigma, cap
\<sn\>	\</\>	Source note (unnumbered footnote)

17. The begin-paragraph code \<p\> is to be used immediately following three blank spaces. See text for full discussion of begin-paragraph and end-paragraph coding options.
18. The word "Preface," to be printed at the top of that section of text.
19. Or arcminute or minute symbol. Do *not* use apostrophe key. These are different symbols in print.

Code	End Code	Description
\<sp\>	None	Special line space[20]
\<sub\>	None	Subscript[21]
\<sup\>	None	Superscript (see note 21)
\<swe\>	None	Swedish slash (see note 2)
\<tau\>	None	Greek tau, lowercase
\<theta\>	None	Greek theta, lowercase
\<THETA\>	None	Greek theta, cap
\<tid\>	None	Tilde accent (see note 2)
\<times\>	None	Multiplication cross ×
\<uc\>	None	Undercircle (see note 2)
\<ud\>	None	Underdot (see note 2)
\<um\>	None	Umlaut (see note 2)
\<upsilon\>	None	Greek upsilon, lowercase
\<UPSILON\>	None	Greek upsilon, cap
\<xi\>	None	Greek xi, lowercase
\<XI\>	None	Greek xi, cap
\<xp\>	\</xp\>	Stop printing and leave space; resume printing (see 2.54)
\<zeta\>	None	Greek zeta, lowercase

20. This code should be used rarely and only in consultation with your publisher. Never, under any circumstances, use it above or below titles, subheads, or extracts.

21. This is a one-time-only code, affecting only the character immediately following it. Hence, for a subscript 12, you must type \<sub\>1\<sub\>2.

Code	End Code	Description
--	None	Em dash (two hyphens, with no space before or after the code--like this)
<3m>	None	3-em dash, sometimes used in reference lists and bibliographies (see 2.101)
<!	!>	Nonprinting comments should be typed between these codes

Select Bibliography

Labuz, Ronald. *How to Typeset from a Word Processor: An Interfacing Guide.* New York and London: R. R. Bowker Co., 1984.

Labuz, Ronald, and Paul Altimonte. *The Interface Data Book for Word Processing/Typesetting: 1984–1985.* New York and London: R. R. Bowker Co., 1984.

Lawrence, John Shelton. *The Electronic Scholar: A Guide to Academic Microcomputing.* Norwood, N.J.: Ablex Publishing, 1984.

Lombardi, John V. *Computer Literacy.* Bloomington: Indiana University Press, 1983.

Myers, Patti. *Telecommunications for Typesetting: A Guide for the User of an Information System.* Arlington, Va.: National Composition Association, 1983.

———. *Typesetting from Magnetic Media: A Guide for the User of an Information System.* Arlington, Va.: National Composition Association, 1984.

Powers, Jack. *Electric Words.* Arlington, Va.: National Composition Association, 1985.

Roth, Stephen F. "Book Publishers Join the Computer Age." *Personal Publishing,* October 1985, 34–35.

———. *The Computer Edge: Microcomputer Trends/Uses in Publishing.* New York and London: R. R. Bowker Co., 1985.

University of Chicago Press. *The Chicago Manual of Style,* 13th ed. Chicago: University of Chicago Press, 1982.

Index

References are to paragraph numbers except where specified otherwise. Specific codes are not indexed here; for a complete list of codes see Appendix D.